RR

PENGUIN CLASSICS

MEDEA AND OTHER PLAYS

EURIPIDES was an Athenian born in 484 B.C. A member of a family of considerable rank, he avoided public duties as far as possible, and devoted his life to the work of a dramatist. His popularity is attested by the survival of seventeen of his plays and by abundant other evidence; though it was partly due to his audience's inability to penetrate the irony of his character-drawing. His unpopularity is equally clear from the constant attacks made upon him in the comedies of Aristophanes, and by the fact that in fifty years he was awarded first prize only four or five times. At the age of seventy-three he found it necessary to leave Athens; he went into voluntary exile at the court of Archelaus, king of Macedon. It was during these last months that he wrote what many consider his greatest work, *The Bacchae*. When the news of his death reached Athens in 406 Sophocles appeared publicly in mourning for him.

PHILIP VELLACOTT has also translated the following volumes for the Penguin Classics: the complete plays of Aeschylus, the complete plays of Euripides, and a volume of Menander and Theophrastus. He was educated at St Paul's School and Magdalene College, Cambridge, and for twenty-four years he taught classics (and drama for twelve years) at Dulwich College. He has lectured on Greek drama on ten tours in the U.S.A., and has spent four terms as Visiting Lecturer in the University of California at Santa Cruz. He is also the author of *Sophocles and Oedipus* (1971), *Ironic Drama: A Study of Euripides' Method and Meaning* (1975), and *The Logic of Tragedy: Morals and Integrity in Aeschylus' Oresteia* (1984).

EURIPIDES

MEDEA
AND OTHER
PLAYS

MEDEA · HECABE · ELECTRA · HERACLES

Translated with an Introduction by
PHILIP VELLACOTT

PENGUIN BOOKS

Penguin Books Ltd, Harmondsworth, Middlesex, England
Viking Penguin Inc., 40 West 23rd Street, New York, New York 10010, U.S.A.
Penguin Books Australia Ltd, Ringwood, Victoria, Australia
Penguin Books Canada Ltd, 2801 John Street, Markham, Ontario, Canada L3R 1B4
Penguin Books (N.Z.) Ltd, 182–190 Wairau Road, Auckland 10, New Zealand

—

This translation first published 1963
Reprinted 1964, 1966, 1968 (twice), 1971, 1972, 1973, 1974, 1975, 1976,
1977, 1978, 1979, 1981, 1982 (twice), 1983, 1984, 1985 (twice), 1986, 1987 (twice)

—

—

Made and printed in Great Britain by
Richard Clay Ltd, Bungay, Suffolk
Set in Monotype Perpetua

The terms for the performance of these plays
may be obtained from
The League of Dramatists,
84 Drayton Gardens, London SW10 9SD,
to whom all applications for permission
should be made

CONTENTS

NTRODUCTION*

MEDEA (431 B.C.)

OF the four plays in this volume, three have in common a point of special interest for their first audience. *Medea*, *Electra*, and *Heracles* are set respectively in Corinth, Argos, and Thebes; but for the solution of their dilemmas, the cleansing of their guilt, they all look to Athens. This observation perhaps illumines one aspect of the unique greatness of Athens. The hypocrisy of neglected ideals has often been condemned as a major sin; but in the moral world as in the romantic, it is better to have loved and lost than never to have loved. The Athenians in their actions were certainly as cruel, as dishonest, as greedy, as revengeful, as irreligious, as other Greeks; but in their thoughts and aspirations many of them loved and honoured justice, integrity, and generosity, and loved their city as the shining embodiment of those virtues – which it was not. Faith without works may be dead – but faith is seldom entirely without works; and the works of the tragedians kept alive the faith of Athenians in the beauty of goodness, and in what their city had sometimes tried to be, even if success had been rare: the sanctuary of Hellas.

In *Electra*, Orestes' guilt was incurred wittingly – but at the command of a god; in *Heracles*, the crime was committed in pure innocence. By contrast, Medea's only excuse was her natural passion for revenge; yet she, no less than the others, could rely on sanctuary in Athens. The Chorus of Corinthian women follow their celebrated hymn of praise for Athens with questions voicing the instinctive protest that there are degrees of wickedness which pollute sanctuary – but that cannot change the story. That this principle of the open gate still had significance in historical times is shown by Thucydides' insistence on it in Pericles' Funeral Speech (in Book ii), where it is stated with pride that Athens allowed free coming and going through her city gates. In *Medea* Euripides' compliment to his city in this hymn of praise appears in some measure to compensate for the effect of the preceding scene.

* A general Introduction to the life and work of Euripides is given in *Alcestis and Other Plays* (Penguin Classics).

INTRODUCTION

The king of Athens and his friendly offer to Medea were part of the
unalterable legend, and would be accepted as such by the Athenian
audience; but the treatment of the episode in this play is not only
curiously arbitrary and unrelated to the rest of the action, but more
than a little satirical; and the figure of Aegeus provides the one flicker
of relief in the otherwise uniform sombreness of the drama.

This, the earliest extant tragedy of Euripides (it is preceded only by
Alcestis), shows a moral pattern similar to that of his last work, *The
Bacchae*. It opens with an oppressed victim claiming the sympathy of
Chorus and audience. As the action develops inevitably, and the
punishment shows itself twice as wicked as the crime, sympathy
changes sides; and we are left with only one comfort, that since the
worst has been reached, there can be no worse thing to follow.

To appreciate the balance of this play, we must take care not to pre-
judge Jason. He was a man of entirely respectable ambitions; and to
these ambitions Medea presented two fatal obstacles: she had involved
him in murder before ever he came to Corinth; and as a non-Greek
she could never be recognized by Greeks as his wife. And the first of
these obstacles is of course part of the reason for the second. Marathon
and Salamis had made the Athenians vividly conscious that the
establishment and growth of civilized values in a barbarous world lay
with them alone as the leaders of Hellenic culture. For Greeks,
'civilized' life meant controlled, orderly, proportionate life, τὸ μηδὲν
ἄγαν, 'No excess'. As a principle this applied equally to everything –
politics, social habits, art. To them it was the only life, and the want of
it a living death. Those who had died for it in the great battles or in
resistance to tyranny were their most honoured heroes. This is the
principle for which Jason stands. If his behaviour strikes us as repellent,
that is how the behaviour of Athenians struck many Greeks of other
States in the days when Athens claimed to be the champion of the
Greek way of life, and the firm opponent of barbarism and all its
ways.

In the great world the forces of civilization are a heroic minority,
and their course is simple enough: to win or die. In a Greek city, such
as the Corinth of this play, the forces of civilization rule, and barbarism appears – here in the person of Medea – as the heroic minority. The play shows a truth which many Greeks must have recognized,
though it was seldom acknowledged in so many words: that when a

8

community or a nation has adopted, in its political and social institutions, the quality of self-control, *sophrosyne*, it soon learns that this quality belongs only in limited measure to its citizens; that the principle of barbarous excess is predominant in most individuals, so that the constant concern of government is to deal with barbarism inside the walls and in the council-chamber, as well as in foreign lands. Just as in the modern world democracy, desperate to resist totalitarianism, resorts to totalitarian methods, weakening its own life in the process, so the fiery Greek temperament made the menace of barbarism the excuse for its own excesses.

In the character of Jason a concern for civilized values is joined with a calculating coldness and an unscrupulous want of feeling. In that of Medea warmth of feeling grows on the same stem as emotional excess and the propensity to violence. Here we see an issue which again is similar to that found in *The Bacchae*. The lesson of both plays is that civilized men ignore at their peril the world of instinct, emotion, and irrational experience; that carefully worked-out notions of right and wrong are dangerous unless they are flexible and allow for constant adjustment. And the ending of *Medea*, with the Sun himself, the source of all life and warmth, vindicating the cause of passion, disorder, violent cruelty, against the cold, orderly, self-protective processes of civilized man, is a reminder that the universe is not on the side of civilization; and that a life combining order with happiness is something men must win for themselves in continual struggle with an unsympathetic environment.

HECABE (425 B.C.)

This play combines two themes, both of which Euripides treated also in other plays. First, the complacent hypocrisy with which men justify cruelty in the name of military or political necessity; second, the tendency of revenge to be more wicked than the crime which provoked it, and thus to forfeit sympathy and the claim of justice. Besides these two themes we have, in the first part, the heroic figure of Polyxena – enough in itself to make the play memorable; and in the second half the vivid interplay of character between Agamemnon and Hecabe. It is a straightforward play for fine actors, offering simple emotion rather than question or conflict.

It has been strongly criticized on the ground that it falls apart into two scarcely connected episodes, concerned respectively with Polyxena and with Polydorus and Polymestor. The same criticism is often levelled at other plays such as *Hippolytus* and *Andromache*, and in some cases reflects a feature of Greek plays which arose inevitably from the restriction of the number of actors to three. In this play, however, that excuse is hardly needed. The play is about ruthless cruelty, and the different results it may produce for both sufferer and spectator. The cruelty of the sentence on Polyxena is transmuted by the heroism of Polyxena herself to an episode of awe-inspiring beauty. The cruelty of Polymestor to Hecabe's son is matured by the reaction of revenge into something profitless and repellent. Not even Agamemnon's verdict can justify Hecabe; for it is so evidently the result of a bad conscience over Polyxena. The whole point of the play lies in the contrast between its two halves; so that to criticize this division is largely irrelevant.

Throughout the action Hecabe is the central figure. The legend said that the accumulation of her sufferings drove her mad, and that she was transformed into a dog. The promontory called Cynossema, the Dog's Tomb, on the coast of the Thracian Chersonese (Gallipoli) was familiar to Greek sailors as the traditional site of Hecabe's burial. The legend itself is a comment on the effect of prolonged anguish on the mind; and this was a subject which greatly occupied Euripides. In this play Hecabe's depth of grief has almost reached the limit of endurance when the action begins. Polyxena's death is made endurable by Polyxena's own nobility; but a further blow is fatal, and Hecabe is transformed into a raving savage.

It has to be remembered that the annihilation of a city was an act which Athens, like other military powers, was capable of deciding on and carrying out. It had been decided on (and revoked at the very last moment) in the case of Mytilene in 427 B.C., two years before the production of this play; it was carried out in the case of Melos in 416 B.C., a year before the production of *The Women of Troy*.* The Greeks were a cruel race, and at the same time an emotional race capable of deep feeling. How much real influence a dramatic poet might exert (necessarily after the event) on the public actions of his city is impossible to estimate; but two pieces of evidence come to mind. One is the scene in the second half of Aristophanes' *The Frogs*, where Aeschylus and

* Included in *The Bacchae and Other Plays* (Penguin Classics).

Euripides are matched against each other for their value to the citizens of Athens. The other is the story of the heavy fine inflicted on Phrynichus (an older contemporary of Aeschylus) for moving his audience to tears with his play about the capture of Miletus. However that may be, the chief interest of this play for modern readers is probably its eloquence and pathos.

ELECTRA (415 B.C.)

Electra has often been a puzzling play for modern readers. This has not prevented if from becoming also one of the most popular in translation, probably because of the striking realism which Euripides here employs both in dialogue and in situation. Many performances, however, must have left English audiences largely in the dark on two points at least: the intended characters of Electra and Orestes, and the significance of the curious recognition-scene. Before examining these in detail we should take a general look at Euripides' treatment of one of the best-known stories in the Troy cycle.

The framework of the story, used also by both Aeschylus and Sophocles, was as follows: before Agamemnon returned from Troy, Electra, fearing that Aegisthus would murder Orestes, had sent him away from Argos to be brought up by Strophius, king of Phocis. Orestes at the time of Agamemnon's murder was about eleven years of age. As soon as he reached manhood he was commanded by the Delphic oracle to go to Argos and avenge his father by killing Clytemnestra and Aegisthus. He reached Argos in disguise, revealed himself to his sister, and with her help accomplished his mission. As a shedder of kindred blood he was then pursued and tormented by the Furies.

Using this material Aeschylus wrote a drama in which the conflict between divine command and moral instinct is fought out in the person of Orestes. Sophocles wrote a dramatic study of Electra as the daughter who turned against her mother that obsession with revenge which she had inherited from her. In these plays the figures of the protagonists are presented on a heroic scale. Though the horror of matricide is recognized, it is not doubted that such a command might have divine sanction. In Euripides' play both Orestes and Electra are far from heroic; the murder of Aegisthus is shown as, at the best, inglorious; that of Clytemnestra as revolting. Yet then, and only then, when brother and sister, having achieved their purpose, stand as the trembling victims of a profitless, relentless, and false tradition of glorious revenge, do we, the audience, feel pity for them.

The obligation and indulgence of revenge played a constant and disastrous part in Greek history, and often gave an unpleasant colour to otherwise attractive characters. This feature of Greek life Euripides sometimes (like Aeschylus) regards as an aspect of the search for ideal justice; more often he presents it as sheer folly, as the principle which perpetuates and aggravates evil and produces no good whatever. In this play he was dealing with a revenge-saga in which long and familiar tradition had upheld the principle in spite of every circumstance of horror. Aeschylus had justified and purified Orestes in the end; Sophocles had never questioned the nobility and justice of his act. Euripides here shows the revenge as conceived and executed in fear and weakness. Orestes, faced with his dilemma, trusts the oracle because he has not the strength to trust his own moral instinct; but neither has he the strength to trust in the rightness of what he has done at Apollo's command. For Euripides, the brutality of this command was a challenge to Orestes, just as the command to sacrifice Iphigenia had been a challenge to his father. Both, being weak, preferred sin under authority to the risks of moral independence.

A crucial point in the interpretation of the whole play is the recognition scene (lines 487–581).* Dispute has often turned on the question why Euripides in this scene should make, as it appears, a detailed criticism of Aeschylus' treatment of the recognition in *The Choephori*, and ridicule the use there made of 'signs' such as the lock of hair and the footprints. This question will be considered presently; but it is a secondary one. The prime question is, Why is the recognition so long delayed and so reluctant? To answer this we must look at clues already given in the early scenes to the characters of Electra and Orestes.

Electra in her opening conversation with the Peasant uses several phrases which suggest that her degradation and grief have led to exaggerated self-pity; and that this indulgence is her one luxury in life. The next scene, Electra's conversation with the Chorus, shows clearly

* For ideas contained in this section I am largely indebted to an illuminating article, 'The Anagnorisis in the *Electra* of Euripides' by David Raeburn (not yet published).

that there is no substance in her complaints that she is without friends
and cut off from social life; and that the squalor of her personal
appearance is a neurotic affectation. Various lines in subsequent scenes
suggest further that she exaggerates the dishonour shown to Agamemnon's body; and that Orestes' slowness in appearing to rescue her is
one of her favourite grievances.

Next let us turn to Orestes. In Electra's imagination her absent
brother is a romantic hero. The suggestion that he might come to
Argos secretly makes her indignant. When Orestes himself enters, he
soon shows that the notion of matricide is a thing he can hardly bear
to put into words. He has not dared to enter the walls of Argos; he is
keeping near the frontier, partly to escape quickly if recognized, partly
to find his sister and consult with her.

Presently their conversation reaches the point where Orestes asks,
'How would Orestes, if he came, react to your situation?' Electra's
answer makes it clear that she expects him to carry out full revenge at
once, and that she herself will go to any length in helping him, even
to the point of killing Clytemnestra with her own hands. Clearly this
is the point where Orestes should reveal himself, so that a plan can be
concerted. He does not reveal himself. Why? It can only be because he
knows that, once Electra recognizes him, he is irrevocably committed
to murdering his mother. Electra will never let him off.

When eventually the Old Man insists on identifying Orestes,
Euripides presents us with a scene in which the chief emotion is
embarrassment. Orestes is consciously reluctant to be recognized
because he sees all too clearly the inevitable consequence; and Electra
is unconsciously reluctant to recognize him because, having for so long
nursed the grievance of his failure to appear, she cannot bear to see
that grievance removed. This tragi-comic situation explains the slowness of the recognition, the nervously foolish remarks of both brother
and sister, and the perfunctory exchange of endearments which
follows.

A further mystery is solved by this interpretation of Euripides' purpose. The traditional features of this story included not only the
Recognition but the 'signs' by which it was effected: the lock of hair,
the footprints, and the piece of cloth, woven by Electra, which
Orestes wore. These signs might or might not be convincing in themselves: they belonged to an early and unsophisticated period, and were

part of the story. To include them *as the means of recognition* would be incongruous with that realistic treatment of the main characters and situation which was to provide the special interest of the play. What Euripides did, therefore, was to make these signs, not the means of recognition, but an ingenious excuse for that delay of recognition which Electra and Orestes, as he conceived them, desired for their own different reasons. And when Electra has rejected all three in theory, she underlines the ambiguity of her attitude by finally accepting a fourth sign – the scar – which has been plainly visible to her for the last half-hour.

The rest of the play needs little comment. In the account of the killing of Aegisthus no detail is spared which could emphasize that Orestes' exploit is not only unheroic but sacrilegious; and Electra's exalted praises, showing that her mental image of her brother is impervious to sordid fact, add an acutely satirical note. After the Messenger's description of the hearty and hospitable Aegisthus, we are introduced to the quiet, chastened, conciliatory figure of Clytemnestra. Electra is unmoved; she will force Orestes to carry out his undertaking to the end, even in face of this defencelessness. Then, as we learn afterwards, at the crucial moment her nerve fails, and she leaves Orestes to do the actual killing. When the deed has been done, brother and sister, who a little while earlier were trying not to know each other, find themselves alone together in a condemning world; and having discovered that each is the other's only friend, they are forced to part.

HERACLES (420 B.C. ?)

The structure of this play is very simple. Neither the course of events nor the interplay of characters provides anything dramatically notable, except for the appearance of immortals in the middle of the play, which will be referred to presently. The story is the vehicle for that straightforward eloquence on the theme of human suffering, of which Euripides was a master. The world presented here is the familiar world where neither birth nor wealth, piety nor courage nor innocence, gives any guarantee against the power of wickedness or the malevolence of chance. What the spirit of man can aim at achieving is a dignity which remains when the gods have withdrawn or joined the side of evil, a serene despair which knows that the world contains no higher hope than the human spirit can find within itself. And in *Heracles* a further encouragement is given: the firmness of human friendship as the one resource available in the depth of suffering. These simple truths are stated with a spacious and satisfying poetic power; and that is the chief interest of the play.

One unusual feature is worth special notice: the sudden and un-expected appearance, half-way through the play, of Iris and Madness. In Euripides supernatural beings, if they appear at all, generally do so at the beginning of a play to explain a situation, or at the end to provide – or offer – a solution. Critics have sometimes censured this appearance in *Heracles* as arbitrary and unmotivated; for Iris simply announces herself as the agent of Hera's jealousy towards Heracles. But the absence of rational motive is surely the dramatist's point. By this visitation he is describing the character, not of any god or human being, but of events themselves, as he observes them occurring in a world which he regards as ruled by Chance – a divinity not only blind but probably malevolent. His description of the world conveys a message entirely different from that of Sophocles. To the questions of a sufferer Sophocles offers one answer: reverence for the unfathomable wisdom and power of Zeus. Euripides wrote for men who had lost that faith, and exhorted them to rely on themselves, and, if they were fortunate, on the loyalty of friends. In this play Amphi-tryon in particular illustrates what must have been the progress of many religiously-minded Athenians, from belief in divine goodness and a rather smug confidence in divine favour, to a conviction that the whole concept of moral goodness begins, operates, and ends in man alone.

This theme is given an unusual kind of confirmation by a passage in the last scene. Theseus, trying to dissuade Heracles from suicide, drags in the somewhat irrelevant argument that gods have often been guilty of unchastity and yet continue to live in Olympus and are not beyond consolation. Heracles replies that he has never believed such stories. These words of Theseus are a curious echo from the Nurse's speech to Phaedra in *Hippolytus*: 'Yet they live in heaven, and show no haste to quit the company of gods. Events have proved too strong for them; and they, believe me, are content.' In *Hippolytus* this argument is used by the Nurse, whose moral attitude is more than dubious, while here it is Theseus who speaks, the godlike hero. In both plays the audience is invited to disbelieve these tales; in *Hippolytus* by the character of the Nurse, here by Heracles' reply. In both cases the implied lesson is that an intelligent man should not rely on the gods for an acceptable standard of moral behaviour, any more than for protection in danger. Man must be his own god, and stand or fall by his own decisions.

Yet another aspect of this kind of 'humanism' is suggested in the same scene. Guilt, and the various ways of dealing with it, are a constant theme of tragedy. Guilt may be punished with death, as in the case of Clytemnestra; or expiated by suffering, as in the case of Orestes; or forgiven by a victim, as in the case of Theseus in *Hippolytus*. What of Heracles' guilt? The modern reader will feel that, since the play clearly shows his madness as sent upon him by divine agency, Heracles is not morally guilty. He himself, however, does not take this view; he knows that he is guilty. But his guilt is not something he can disown; it is a part of his life, which from beginning to end has been a life of violence. Heracles looks at the famous bow which has brought him victory in so many struggles, and has now killed his wife and children. Is he to take it with him to Athens? Or must he abandon it? 'Never! This bow is anguish to me, yet I cannot part with it.' He is Heracles, and can never be any other man; even the madness which came on him is a part of his nature which he must recognize and learn to live with. He is himself the only person who has the right to forgive what he has done. He knows himself; he will keep his bow.

The title of this play is given in some MSS. as 'Heracles Mainomenos', 'The Madness of Heracles'. The addition may have been made to distinguish it in reference from 'The Heracleidae', 'The Children of Heracles'. Most modern editors call it 'Hercules Furens', which is an unnecessary Latinism. Latinism in Hellene affairs is almost always to be deplored.

MEDEA

*

John Hausman

Characters:

- NURSE
- TUTOR *to Medea's sons*
- MEDEA
- CHORUS *of Corinthian women*
- CREON, *king of Corinth*
- JASON
- AEGEUS, *king of Athens*
- MESSENGER
- MEDEA'S TWO CHILDREN

*

Scene: Before Jason's house in Corinth

NURSE: If only they had never gone! If the Argo's hull
Never had winged out through the grey-blue jaws of rock
And on towards Colchis! If that pine on Pelion's slopes
Had never felt the axe, and fallen, to put oars
Into those heroes' hands, who went at Pelias' bidding
To fetch the golden fleece! Then neither would Medea,
My mistress, ever have set sail for the walled town
Of Iolcus, mad with love for Jason; nor would she,
When Pelias' daughters, at her instance, killed their father,
Have come with Jason and her children to live here
In Corinth; where, coming as an exile, she has earned
The citizens' welcome; while to Jason she is all
Obedience — and in marriage that's the saving thing,
When a wife obediently accepts her husband's will.

But now her world has turned to enmity, and wounds her
Where her affection's deepest. Jason has betrayed

17

His own sons, and my mistress, for a royal bed,
For alliance with the king of Corinth. He has married
Glauce, Creon's daughter. Poor Medea! Scorned and shamed,
She raves, invoking every vow and solemn pledge
That Jason made her, and calls the gods as witnesses
What thanks she has received for her fidelity.
She will not eat; she lies collapsed in agony,
Dissolving the long hours in tears. Since first she heard
Of Jason's wickedness, she has not raised her eyes,
Or moved her cheek from the hard ground; and when her
     friends
Reason with her, she might be a rock or wave of the sea,
For all she hears – unless, maybe, she turns away
Her lovely head, speaks to herself alone, and wails
Aloud for her dear father, her own land and home,
Which she betrayed and left, to come here with this man
Who now spurns and insults her. Poor Medea! Now
She learns through pain what blessings they enjoy who are not
Uprooted from their native land. She hates her sons:
To see them is no pleasure to her. I am afraid
Some dreadful purpose is forming in her mind. She is
A frightening woman; no one who makes an enemy
Of her will carry off an easy victory.

Here come the boys, back from their running. They've no
     thought
Of this cruel blow that's fallen on their mother. Well,
They're young; young heads and painful thoughts don't go
     together.
          Enter the TUTOR *with* MEDEA'S TWO SONS.
TUTOR: Old nurse and servant of my mistress's house, tell me,
     What are you doing, standing out here by the door,
     All alone, talking to yourself, harping on trouble?
     Eh? What does Medea say to being left alone?
NURSE: Old friend, tutor of Jason's sons, an honest slave

Suffers in her own heart the blow that strikes her mistress.
It was too much, I couldn't bear it; I had to come
Out here and tell my mistress's wrongs to earth and heaven.
TUTOR: Poor woman! Has she not stopped crying yet?
NURSE: Stopped crying?
I envy you. Her grief's just born – not yet half-grown.
TUTOR: Poor fool – though she's my mistress and I shouldn't
    say it –
She had better save her tears. She has not heard the worst.
NURSE: The worst? What now? Don't keep it from me. What
    has happened?
TUTOR: Why, nothing's happened. I'm sorry I said anything.
NURSE: Look – we're both slaves together: don't keep me in
    the dark.
Is it so great a secret? I can hold my tongue.
TUTOR: I'd gone along to the benches where the old men play
At dice, next to the holy fountain of Peirene;
They thought I was not listening; and I heard one say
That Creon king of Corinth means to send these boys
Away from here – to banish them, and their mother too.
Whether the story's true I don't know. I hope not.
NURSE: But surely Jason won't stand by and see his sons
Banished, even if he has a quarrel with their mother?
TUTOR: Old love is ousted by new love. Jason's no friend
To this house.
NURSE: Then we're lost, if we must add new trouble
To old, before we're rid of what we had already.
TUTOR: But listen: it's no time to tell Medea this.
Keep quiet, say nothing about it.
NURSE: Children, do you hear
What sort of father Jason is to you? My curse
On – No! No curse; he is my master. All the same,
He is guilty: he has betrayed those near and dear to him.
TUTOR: What man's not guilty? It's taken you a long time to
    learn

That everybody loves himself more than his neighbour.
These boys are nothing to their father: he's in love.

NURSE: Run into the house, boys. Everything will be all
    right.

            [*The children move away a little.*]
You do your best to keep them by themselves, as long
As she's in this dark mood; don't let them go to her.
I've watched her watching them, her eye like a wild bull's.
There's something that she means to do; and I know this:
She'll not relax her rage till it has found its victim.
God grant she strike her enemies and not her friends!

            MEDEA'S *voice is heard from inside the house.*

MEDEA: Oh, oh! What misery, what wretchedness!
    What shall I do? If only I were dead!

NURSE: There! You can hear; it is your mother
    Racking her heart, racking her anger.
    Quick, now, children, hurry indoors;
    And don't go within sight of her,
    Or anywhere near her; keep a safe distance.
    Her mood is cruel, her nature dangerous,
    Her will fierce and intractable.
    Come on, now, in with you both at once.

        [*The* CHILDREN *go in, and the* TUTOR *follows.*]
    The dark cloud of her lamentations
    Is just beginning. Soon, I know,
    It will burst aflame as her anger rises.
    Deep in passion and unrelenting,
    What will she do now, stung with insult?

MEDEA [*indoors*]: Do I not suffer? Am I not wronged? Should
    I not weep?
    Children, your mother is hated, and you are cursed:
    Death take you, with your father, and perish his whole
        house!

NURSE: Oh, the pity of it! Poor Medea!
    Your children – why, what have *they* to do

With their father's wickedness? Why hate *them*?
I am sick with fear for you, children, terror
Of what may happen. The mind of a queen
Is a thing to fear. A queen is used
To giving commands, not obeying them;
And her rage once roused is hard to appease.

To have learnt to live on the common level
Is better. No grand life for me,
Just peace and quiet as I grow old.
The middle way, neither great nor mean,
Is best by far, in name and practice.
To be rich and powerful brings no blessing;
Only more utterly
Is the prosperous house destroyed, when the gods are angry.

Enter the CHORUS *of Corinthian women.*

CHORUS:
    I heard her voice, I heard
    ' That unhappy woman from Colchis
    Still crying, not calm yet.
    Old Nurse, tell us about her.
    As I stood by the door I heard her
    Crying inside the palace.
    And my own heart suffers too
    When Jason's house is suffering;
    For that is where my loyalty lies.

NURSE: Jason's house? It no longer exists; all that is finished.
    Jason is a prisoner in a princess's bed;
    And Medea is in her room
    Melting her life away in tears;
    No word from any friend can give her comfort.

MEDEA [*still from indoors*]:
    Come, flame of the sky,
    Pierce through my head!
    What do I gain from living any longer?

Oh, how I hate living! I want
To end my life, leave it behind, and die.

CHORUS:

O Zeus, and Earth, and Light,
Do you hear the chanted prayer
Of a wife in her anguish?

> [*turning to the door and addressing* MEDEA]

What madness is this? The bed you long for –
Is it what others shrink from?
Is it death you demand?
Do not pray that prayer, Medea!
If your husband is won to a new love –
The thing is common; why let it anger you?
Zeus will plead your cause.
Check this passionate grief over your husband
Which wastes you away.

MEDEA: Mighty Themis! Dread Artemis!
Do you see how I am used –
In spite of those great oaths I bound him with –
By my accursed husband?
Oh, may I see Jason and his bride
Ground to pieces in their shattered palace
For the wrong they have dared to do to me, unprovoked!
O my father, my city, you I deserted;
My brother I shamefully murdered!

NURSE: Do you hear what my mistress is saying,
Clamouring to Themis, hearer of prayer,
And to Zeus, who is named guardian of men's oaths?
It is no trifling matter
That can end a rage like hers.

CHORUS: I wish she would come out here and let us see her
And talk to her; if she would listen
Perhaps she would drop this fierce resentful spirit,
This passionate indignation.
As a friend I am anxious to do whatever I can.

Go, nurse, persuade her to come out to us.
Tell her we are all on her side.
Hurry, before she does harm – to those in there;
This passion of hers is an irresistible flood.
NURSE: I will. I fear I shall not persuade her;
Still, I am glad to do my best.
Yet as soon as any of us servants
Goes near to her, or tries to speak,
She glares at us like a mad bull
Or a lioness guarding her cubs.

[*The* NURSE *goes to the door, where she turns.*]

The men of old times had little sense;
If you called them fools you wouldn't be far wrong.
They invented songs, and all the sweetness of music,
To perform at feasts, banquets, and celebrations;
But no one thought of using
Songs and stringed instruments
To banish the bitterness and pain of life.
Sorrow is the real cause
Of deaths and disasters and families destroyed.
If music could cure sorrow it would be precious;
But after a good dinner why sing songs?
When people have fed full they're happy already.

The NURSE *goes in.*

CHORUS:
I heard her sobbing and wailing,
Shouting shrill, pitiful accusations
Against her husband who has betrayed her.
She invokes Themis, daughter of Zeus,
Who witnessed those promises which drew her
Across from Asia to Hellas, setting sail at night,
Threading the salt strait,
Key and barrier to the Pontic Sea.

MEDEA *comes out. She is not shaken with weeping, but cool and
self-possessed.*

23

MEDEA: Women of Corinth, I would not have you censure me,
So I have come. Many, I know, are proud at heart,
Indoors or out; but others are ill spoken of
As supercilious, just because their ways are quiet.
There is no justice in the world's censorious eyes.
They will not wait to learn a man's true character;
Though no wrong has been done them, one look – and they
    hate.
Of course a stranger must conform; even a Greek
Should not annoy his fellows by crass stubbornness.
I accept my place; but this blow that has fallen on me
Was not to be expected. It has crushed my heart.
Life has no pleasure left, dear friends. I want to die.
Jason was my whole life; he knows that well. Now he
Has proved himself the most contemptible of men.

Surely, of all creatures that have life and will, we women
Are the most wretched. When, for an extravagant sum,
We have bought a husband, we must then accept him as
Possessor of our body. This is to aggravate
Wrong with worse wrong. Then the great question: will the
    man
We get be bad or good? For women, divorce is not
Respectable; to repel the man, not possible.

Still more, a foreign woman, coming among new laws,
New customs, needs the skill of magic, to find out
What her home could not teach her, how to treat the man
Whose bed she shares. And if in this exacting toil
We are successful, and our husband does not struggle
Under the marriage yoke, our life is enviable.
Otherwise, death is better. If a man grows tired
Of the company at home, he can go out, and find
A cure for tediousness. We wives are forced to look
To one man only. And, they tell us, we at home

Live free from danger, they go out to battle: fools!
I'd rather stand three times in the front line than bear
One child.

　　　　　But the same arguments do not apply
To you and me. You have this city, your father's home,
The enjoyment of your life, and your friends' company.
I am alone; I have no city; now my husband
Insults me. I was taken as plunder from a land
At the earth's edge. I have no mother, brother, nor any
Of my own blood to turn to in this extremity.

So, I make one request. If I can find a way
To work revenge on Jason for his wrongs to me,
Say nothing. A woman's weak and timid in most matters;
The noise of war, the look of steel, makes her a coward.
But touch her right in marriage, and there's no bloodier
　　spirit.

CHORUS: I'll do as you ask. To punish Jason will be just.
　　I do not wonder that you take such wrongs to heart.
　　　　　　　　[CREON approaches.]
　　But look, Medea; I see Creon, King of Corinth;
　　He must have come to tell you of some new decision.

CREON: You there, Medea, scowling rage against your hus-
　　band!
　　I order you out of Corinth; take your sons and go
　　Into exile. Waste no time; I'm here to see this order
　　Enforced. And I'm not going back into my palace
　　Until I've put you safe outside my boundaries.

MEDEA: Oh! this is the cruel end of my accursed life!
　　My enemies have spread full sail; no welcoming shore
　　Waits to receive and save me. Ill-treated as I am,
　　Creon, I ask: for what offence do you banish me?

CREON: I fear you. Why wrap up the truth? I fear that you
　　May do my daughter some irreparable harm.
　　A number of things contribute to my anxiety.

You're a clever woman, skilled in many evil arts;
You're barred from Jason's bed, and that enrages you.
I learn too from reports, that you have uttered threats
Of revenge on Jason and his bride and his bride's father.
I'll act first, then, in self-defence. I'd rather make you
My enemy now, than weaken, and later pay with tears.

MEDEA: My reputation, yet again! Many times, Creon,
It has been my curse and ruin. A man of any shrewdness
Should never have his children taught to use their brains
More than their fellows. What do you gain by being clever?
You neglect your own affairs; and all your fellow citizens
Hate you. Those who are fools will call you ignorant
And useless, when you offer them unfamiliar knowledge.
As for those thought intelligent, if people rank
You above *them*, that is a thing they will not stand.
I know this from experience: because I am clever,
They are jealous; while the rest dislike me. After all,
I am not so clever as all that.

　　　　　　　　　　So you, Creon,
Are afraid – of what? Some harm that I might do to you?
Don't let *me* alarm you, Creon. I'm in no position –
A woman – to wrong a king. You have done me no wrong.
You've given your daughter to the man you chose. I hate
My husband – true; but you had every right to do
As you have done. So now I bear no grudge against
Your happiness: marry your daughter to him, and good luck
To you both. But let me live in Corinth. I will bear
My wrongs in silence, yielding to superior strength.

CREON: Your words are gentle; but my blood runs cold to
　　　think
What plots you may be nursing deep within your heart.
In fact, I trust you so much less now than before.
A woman of hot temper – and a man the same –
Is a less dangerous enemy than one quiet and clever.
So out you go, and quickly; no more arguing.

I've made my mind up; you're my enemy. No craft
Of yours will find a way of staying in my city.

MEDEA: I kneel to you, I beseech you by the young bride, your
child.

CREON: You're wasting words; you'll never make me change
my mind.

MEDEA: I beg you! Will you cast off pity, and banish me?

CREON: I will: I have more love for my family than for you.

MEDEA: My home, my country! How my thoughts turn to you
now!

CREON: I love my country too – next only to my daughter.

MEDEA: Oh, what an evil power love has in people's lives!

CREON: That would depend on circumstances, I imagine.

MEDEA: Great Zeus, remember who caused all this suffering!

CREON: Go, you poor wretch, take all my troubles with you!
Go!

MEDEA: I know what trouble is; I have no need of more.

CREON: In a moment you'll be thrown out neck and crop.
Here, men!

MEDEA: No, no, not that! But, Creon, I have one thing to ask.

CREON: You seem inclined, Medea, to give me trouble still.

MEDEA: I'll go. [*She still clings to him.*] It was not *that* I begged.

CREON: Then why resist?
Why will you not get out?

MEDEA: This one day let me stay,
To settle some plan for my exile, make provision
For my two sons, since their own father is not concerned
To help them. Show some pity: you are a father too,
You should feel kindly towards them. For myself, exile
Is nothing. I weep for them; their fate is very hard.

CREON: I'm no tyrant by nature. My soft heart has often
Betrayed me; and I know it's foolish of me now;
Yet none the less, Medea, you shall have what you ask.
But take this warning: if tomorrow's holy sun
Finds you or them inside my boundaries, you die.

That is my solemn word. Now stay here, if you must,
This one day. You can hardly in one day accomplish
What I am afraid of.

Exit CREON.

CHORUS:
  Medea, poor Medea!
  Your grief touches our hearts.
  A wanderer, where can you turn?
  To what welcoming house?
  To what protecting land?
  How wild with dread and danger
  Is the sea where the gods have set your course!

MEDEA: A bad predicament all round – yes, true enough;
  But don't imagine things will end as they are now.
  Trials are yet to come for this new-wedded pair;
  Nor shall those nearest to them get off easily.

  Do you think I would ever have fawned so on this man,
  Except to gain my purpose, carry out my schemes?
  Not one touch, not one word: yet he – oh, what a fool!
  By banishing me at once he could have thwarted me
  Utterly; instead, he allows me to remain one day.
  Today three of my enemies I shall strike dead:
  Father and daughter; and *my* husband.

  I have in mind so many paths of death for them,
  I don't know which to choose. Should I set fire to the house,
  And burn the bridal chamber? Or creep up to their bed
  And drive a sharp knife through their guts? There is one
      fear:
  If I am caught entering the house, or in the act,
  I die, and the last laugh goes to my enemies.
  The best is the direct way, which most suits my bent:
  To kill by poison.

So – say they are dead: what city will receive me then?
What friend will guarantee my safety, offer land
And home as sanctuary? None. I'll wait a little.
If some strong tower of help appears, I'll carry out
This murder cunningly and quietly. But if Fate
Banishes me without resource, I will myself
Take sword in hand, harden my heart to the uttermost,
And kill them both, even if I am to die for it.

For, by Queen Hecate, whom above all divinities
I venerate, my chosen accomplice, to whose presence
My central hearth is dedicated, no one of them
Shall hurt me and not suffer for it! Let me work:
In bitterness and pain they shall repent this marriage,
Repent their houses joined, repent my banishment.

Come! Lay your plan, Medea; scheme with all your skill.
On to the deadly moment that shall test your nerve!
You see now where you stand. Your father was a king,
His father was the Sun-god: you must not invite
Laughter from Jason and his new allies, the tribe
Of Sisyphus. You know what you must do. Besides –
                    [*She turns to the Chorus.*]
We were born women – useless for honest purposes,
But in all kinds of evil skilled practitioners.
CHORUS: Streams of the sacred rivers flow uphill;
    Tradition, order, all things are reversed:
        Deceit is *men*'s device now,
        Men's oaths are gods' dishonour.
    Legend will now reverse our reputation;
    A time comes when the female sex is honoured;
        That old discordant slander
        Shall no more hold us subject.
    Male poets of past ages, with their ballads
    Of faithless women, shall go out of fashion;

29

For Phoebus, Prince of Music,
Never bestowed the lyric inspiration
  Through female understanding –
  Or we'd find themes for poems,
We'd counter with our epics against man.
Oh, Time is old; and in his store of tales
  Men figure no less famous
  Or infamous than women.

So you, Medea, wild with love,
Set sail from your father's house,
Threading the Rocky Jaws of the eastern sea;
And here, living in a strange country,
Your marriage lost, your bed solitary,
You are driven beyond the borders,
An exile with no redress.
The grace of sworn oaths is gone;
Honour remains no more
In the wide Greek world, but is flown to the sky.
Where can you turn for shelter?
Your father's door is closed against you;
Another is now mistress of your husband's bed;
A new queen rules in your house.

Enter JASON.

JASON: I have often noticed – this is not the first occasion –
What fatal results follow from ungoverned rage.
You could have stayed in Corinth, still lived in this house,
If you had quietly accepted the decisions
Of those in power. Instead, you talked like a fool; and
    now
You are banished. Well, your angry words don't upset *me*;
Go on as long as you like reciting Jason's crimes.
But after your abuse of the King and the princess
Think yourself lucky to be let off with banishment.
I have tried all the time to calm them down; but you

30

Would not give up your ridiculous tirades against
The royal family. So, you're banished. However, I
Will not desert a friend. I have carefully considered
Your problem, and come now, in spite of everything,
To see that you and the children are not sent away
With an empty purse, or unprovided. Exile brings
With it a train of difficulties. You no doubt
Hate me: but I could never bear ill-will to you.

MEDEA: You filthy coward! – if I knew any worse name
For such unmanliness I'd use it – so, you've come!
You, my worst enemy, come to me! Oh, it's not courage,
This looking friends in the face after betraying them.
It is not even audacity; it's a disease,
The worst a man can have, pure shamelessness. However,
It is as well you came; to say what I have to say
Will ease my heart; to hear it said will make you wince.

I will begin at the beginning. When you were sent
To master the fire-breathing bulls, yoke them, and sow
The deadly furrow, then I saved your life; and that
Every Greek who sailed with you in the Argo knows.
The serpent that kept watch over the Golden Fleece,
Coiled round it fold on fold, unsleeping – it was I
Who killed it, and so lit the torch of your success.
I willingly deceived my father; left my home;
With you I came to Iolcus by Mount Pelion,
Showing much love and little wisdom. There I put
King Pelias to the most horrible of deaths
By his own daughters' hands, and ruined his whole house.
And in return for this you have the wickedness
To turn me out, to get yourself another wife,
Even after I had borne you sons! If you had still
Been childless I could have pardoned you for hankering
After this new marriage. But respect for oaths has gone
To the wind. Do you, I wonder, think that the old gods

31

No longer rule? Or that new laws are now in force?
You must know you are guilty of perjury to me.

My poor right hand, which you so often clasped! My knees
Which you then clung to! How we are besmirched and
    mocked
By this man's broken vows, and all our hopes deceived!

Come, I'll ask your advice as if you were a friend.
Not that I hope for any help from you; but still,
I'll ask you, and expose your infamy. Where now
Can I turn? Back to my country and my father's house,
Which I betrayed to come with you? Or to Iolcus,
To Pelias's wretched daughters? What a welcome they
Would offer me, who killed their father! Thus it stands:
My friends at home now hate me; and in helping you
I have earned the enmity of those I had no right
To hurt. For my reward, you have made me the envy
Of Hellene women everywhere! A marvellous
Husband I have, and faithful too, in the name of pity;
When I'm banished, thrown out of the country without a
    friend,
Alone with my forlorn waifs. Yes, a shining shame
It will be to you, the new-made bridegroom, that your own
    sons,
And I who saved your life, are begging beside the road!

O Zeus! Why have you given us clear signs to tell
True gold from counterfeit; but when we need to know
Bad *men* from good, the flesh bears no revealing mark?
CHORUS: The fiercest anger of all, the most incurable,
    Is that which rages in the place of dearest love.
JASON: I have to show myself a clever speaker, it seems.
    This hurricane of recrimination and abuse
    Calls for good seamanship: I'll furl all but an inch

32

Of sail, and ride it out. To begin with, since you build
To such a height your services to me, I hold
That credit for my successful voyage was solely due
To Aphrodite, no one else divine or human.
I admit, you have intelligence; but, to recount
How helpless passion drove you then to save my life
Would be invidious; and I will not stress the point.
Your services, so far as they went, were well enough;
But in return for saving me you got far more
Than you gave. Allow me, in the first place, to point out
That you left a barbarous land to become a resident
Of Hellas; here you have known justice; you have lived
In a society where force yields place to law.
Moreover, here your gifts are widely recognized,
You are famous; if you still lived at the ends of the earth
Your name would never be spoken. Personally, unless
Life brings me fame, I long neither for hoards of gold,
Nor for a voice sweeter than Orpheus! – Well, *you* began
The argument about my voyage; and that's my answer.

As for your scurrilous taunts against my marriage with
The royal family, I shall show you that my action
Was wise, not swayed by passion, and directed towards
Your interests and my children's. – No, keep quiet! When I
Came here from Iolcus as a stateless exile, dogged
And thwarted by misfortunes – why, what luckier chance
Could I have met, than marriage with the King's daughter?
It was not, as you resentfully assume, that I
Found your attractions wearisome, and was smitten with
Desire for a new wife; nor did I specially want
To raise a numerous family – the sons we have
Are enough, I'm satisfied; but I wanted to ensure
First – and the most important – that we should live well
And not be poor; I know how a poor man is shunned
By all his friends. Next, that I could bring up my sons

In a manner worthy of my descent; have other sons,
Perhaps, as brothers to your children; give them all
An equal place, and so build up a closely-knit
And prosperous family. *You* need no more children, do you?
While *I* thought it worth while to ensure advantages
For those I have, by means of those I hope to have.

Was such a plan, then, wicked? Even you would approve
If you could govern your sex-jealousy. But you women
Have reached a state where, if all's well with your sex-life,
You've everything you wish for; but when *that* goes wrong,
At once all that is best and noblest turns to gall.
If only children could be got some other way,
Without the female sex! If women didn't exist,
Human life would be rid of all its miseries.

CHORUS: Jason, you have set your case forth very plausibly.
But to my mind – though you may be surprised at this –
You are acting wrongly in thus abandoning your wife.

MEDEA: No doubt I differ from many people in many ways.
To me, a wicked man who is also eloquent
Seems the most guilty of them all. He'll cut your throat
As bold as brass, because he knows he can dress up murder
In handsome words. He's not so clever after all.
You dare outface me now with glib high-mindedness!
One word will throw you: if you were honest, you ought
first
To have won me over, not got married behind my back.

JASON: No doubt, if I had mentioned it, you would have
proved
Most helpful. Why, even now you will not bring yourself
To calm this raging temper.

MEDEA: That was not the point;
But you're an ageing man, and an Asiatic wife
Was no longer respectable.

JASON: Understand this:

34

It's not for the sake of any woman that I have made
This royal marriage, but, as I've already said,
To ensure your future, and to give my children brothers
Of royal blood, and build security for us all.

MEDEA: I loathe your prosperous future; I'll have none of
it,
Nor none of your security – it galls my heart.

JASON: You know – you'll change your mind and be more
sensible.
You'll soon stop thinking good is bad, and striking these
Pathetic poses when in fact you're fortunate.

MEDEA: Go on, insult me: you have a roof over your head.
I am alone, an exile.

JASON: It was your own choice.
Blame no one but yourself

MEDEA: *My* choice? What did I do?
Did I make you my wife and then abandon you?

JASON: You called down wicked curses on the King and his
house.

MEDEA: I did. On your house too Fate sends me as a curse.

JASON: I'll not pursue this further. If there's anything else
I can provide to meet the children's needs or yours,
Tell me; I'll gladly give whatever you want, or send
Letters of introduction, if you like, to friends
Who will help you. – Listen: to refuse such help is mad.
You've everything to gain if you give up this rage.

MEDEA: Nothing would induce me to have dealings with your
friends,
Nor to take any gift of yours; so offer none.
A lying traitor's gifts carry no luck.

JASON: Very well.
I call the gods to witness that I have done my best
To help you and the children. You make no response
To kindness; friendly overtures you obstinately
Reject. So much the worse for you.

MEDEA: Go! You have spent
   Too long out here. You are consumed with craving for
   Your newly-won bride. Go, enjoy her!
                   [*Exit* JASON.]
                              It may be –
   And God uphold my words – that this your marriage-day
   Will end with marriage lost, loathing and horror left.

CHORUS:
      Visitations of love that come
      Raging and violent on a man
      Bring him neither good repute nor goodness.
      But if Aphrodite descends in gentleness
      No other goddess brings such delight.
      Never, Queen Aphrodite,
      Loose against me from your golden bow,
      Dipped in sweetness of desire,
      Your inescapable arrow!

      Let Innocence, the gods' loveliest gift,
      Choose me for her own;
      Never may the dread Cyprian
      Craze my heart to leave old love for new,
      Sending to assault me
      Angry disputes and feuds unending;
      But let her judge shrewdly the loves of women
      And respect the bed where no war rages.

      O my country, my home!
      May the gods save me from becoming
      A stateless refugee
      Dragging out an intolerable life
      In desperate helplessness!
      That is the most pitiful of all griefs;
      Death is better. Should such a day come to me
      I pray for death first.

Of all pains and hardships none is worse
Than to be deprived of your native land.

This is no mere reflection derived from hearsay;
It is something we have seen.
You, Medea, have suffered the most shattering of blows;
Yet neither the city of Corinth
Nor any friend has taken pity on you.
May dishonour and ruin fall on the man
Who, having unlocked the secrets
Of a friend's frank heart, can then disown him!
He shall be no friend of mine.

Enter AEGEUS.

AEGEUS: All happiness to you, Medea! Between old friends
There is no better greeting.

MEDEA: All happiness to you,
Aegeus, son of Pandion the wise! Where have you come
from?

AEGEUS: From Delphi, from the ancient oracle of Apollo.

MEDEA: The centre of the earth, the home of prophecy:
Why did you go?

AEGEUS: To ask for children; that my seed
May become fertile.

MEDEA: Why, have you lived so many years
Childless?

AEGEUS: Childless I am; so some fate has ordained.

MEDEA: You have a wife, or not?

AEGEUS: I am married.

MEDEA: And what answer
Did Phoebus give you about children?

AEGEUS: His answer was
Too subtle for me or any human interpreter.

MEDEA: Is it lawful for me to hear it?

AEGEUS: Certainly; a brain
Like yours is what is needed.

MEDEA: Tell me, since you may.

AEGEUS: He commanded me 'not to unstop the wineskin's neck' –

MEDEA: Yes – until when?

AEGEUS: Until I came safe home again.

MEDEA: I see. And for what purpose have you sailed to Corinth?

AEGEUS: You know the King of Troezen, Pittheus, son of Pelops?

MEDEA: Yes, a most pious man.

AEGEUS: I want to ask his advice
About this oracle.

MEDEA: He is an expert in such matters.

AEGEUS: Yes, and my closest friend. We went to the wars together.

MEDEA: I hope you will get all you long for, and be happy.

AEGEUS: But you are looking pale and wasted: what is the matter?

MEDEA: Aegeus, my husband's the most evil man alive.

AEGEUS: Why, what's this? Tell me all about your unhappiness.

MEDEA: Jason has betrayed me, though I never did him wrong.

AEGEUS: What has he done? Explain exactly.

MEDEA: He has taken
Another wife, and made her mistress of *my* house.

AEGEUS: But such a thing is shameful! He has never dared –

MEDEA: It is so. Once he loved me; now I am disowned.

AEGEUS: Was he tired of you? Or did he fall in love elsewhere?

MEDEA: Oh, passionately. He's not a man his friends can trust.

AEGEUS: Well, if – as you say – he's a bad lot, let him go.

MEDEA: It's royalty and power he's fallen in love with.

AEGEUS   What?
Go on. Who's the girl's father?

MEDEA: Creon, King of Corinth.

AEGEUS: I see. Then you have every reason to be upset.

MEDEA: It is the end of everything! What's more, I'm banished.

AEGEUS: Worse still – extraordinary! Why, who has banished
   you?

MEDEA: Creon has banished me from Corinth.

AEGEUS: And does Jason
   Accept this? How disgraceful!

MEDEA: Oh, no! He protests.
   But he's resolved to bear it bravely. – Aegeus, see,
   I touch your beard as a suppliant, embrace your knees,
   Imploring you to have pity on my wretchedness.
   Have pity! I am an exile; let me not be friendless.
   Receive me in Athens; give me a welcome in your house.
   So may the gods grant you fertility, and bring
   Your life to a happy close. You have not realized
   What good luck chance has brought you. I know certain
      drugs
   Whose power will put an end to your sterility.
   I promise you shall beget children.

AEGEUS: I am anxious,
   For many reasons, to help you in this way, Medea;
   First, for the gods' sake, then this hope you've given me
   Of children – for I've quite despaired of my own powers.
   This then is what I'll do: once you can get to Athens
   I'll keep my promise and protect you all I can.
   But I must make this clear first: I do not intend
   To take you with me away from Corinth. If you come
   Yourself to Athens, you shall have sanctuary there;
   I will not give you up to anyone. But first
   Get clear of Corinth without help; the Corinthians too
   Are friends of mine, and I don't wish to give offence.

MEDEA: So be it. Now confirm your promise with an oath,
   And all is well between us.

AEGEUS: Why? Do you not trust me?
   What troubles you?

MEDEA: I trust you; but I have enemies –

39

Not only Creon, but the house of Pelias.
Once you are bound by oaths you will not give me up
If they should try to take me out of your territory.
But if your promise is verbal, and not sworn to the gods,
Perhaps you will make friends with them, and agree to do
What they demand. I've no power on my side, while they
Have wealth and all the resources of a royal house.

AEGEUS: Your forethought is remarkable; but since you
     wish it
I've no objection. In fact, the taking of an oath
Safeguards me; since I can confront your enemies
With a clear excuse; while *you* have full security.
So name your gods.

MEDEA: Swear by the Earth under your feet,
By the Sun, my father's father, and the whole race of gods.

AEGEUS: Tell me what I shall swear to do or not to do.

MEDEA: Never yourself to expel me from your territory;
And, if my enemies want to take me away, never
Willingly, while you live, to give me up to them.

AEGEUS: I swear by Earth, and by the burning light of the
     Sun,
And all the gods, to keep the words you have just spoken.

MEDEA: I am satisfied. And if you break your oath, what then?

AEGEUS: Then may the gods do to me as to all guilty men.

MEDEA: Go now, and joy be with you. Everything is well.
I'll reach your city as quickly as I can, when I
Have carried out my purpose and achieved my wish.

          AEGEUS *clasps her hand and hurries off.*

CHORUS: May Hermes, protector of travellers, bring you
Safe to your home, Aegeus; may you accomplish
All that you so earnestly desire;
For your noble heart wins our goodwill.

MEDEA: O Zeus! O Justice, daughter of Zeus! O glorious
     Sun!
Now I am on the road to victory; now there's hope!

I shall see my enemies punished as they deserve.
Just where my plot was weakest, at that very point
Help has appeared in this man Aegeus; he is a haven
Where I shall find safe mooring, once I reach the walls
Of the city of Athens. Now I'll tell you all my plans:
They'll not make pleasant hearing.

[*Medea's* NURSE *has entered; she listens in silence.*]

                                        First I'll send a slave
To Jason, asking him to come to me; and then
I'll give him soft talk; tell him he has acted well,
Tell him I think this royal marriage which he has bought
With my betrayal is for the best and wisely planned.
But I shall beg that my children be allowed to stay.
Not that I would think of leaving sons of mine behind
On enemy soil for those who hate me to insult;
But in my plot to kill the princess they must help.
I'll send them to the palace bearing gifts, a dress
Of soft weave and a coronet of beaten gold.
If she takes and puts on this finery, both she
And all who touch her will expire in agony;
With such a deadly poison I'll anoint my gifts.

However, enough of that. What makes me cry with pain
Is the next thing I have to do. I will kill my sons.
No one shall take my children from me. When I have made
Jason's whole house a shambles, I will leave Corinth
A murderess, flying from my darling children's blood.
Yes, I can endure guilt, however horrible;
The laughter of my enemies I will not endure.

Now let things take their course. What use is life to me?
I have no land, no home, no refuge from despair.
My folly was committed long ago, when I
Was ready to desert my father's house, won over
By eloquence from a Greek, whom with God's help I now

Will punish. He shall never see alive again
The sons he had from me. From his new bride he never
Shall breed a son; she by my poison, wretched girl,
Must die a hideous death. Let no one think of me
As humble or weak or passive; let them understand
I am of a different kind: dangerous to my enemies,
Loyal to my friends. To such a life glory belongs.

CHORUS: Since you have told us everything, and since I want
To be your friend, and also to uphold the laws
Of human life – I tell you, you must not do this!

MEDEA: No other thing is possible. You have excuse
For speaking so: you have not been treated as I have.

CHORUS: But – to kill your own children! Can you steel your
heart?

MEDEA: This is the way to deal Jason the deepest wound.

CHORUS: This way will bring you too the deepest misery.

MEDEA: Let be. Until it is done words are unnecessary.
Nurse! You are the one I use for messages of trust.
Go and bring Jason here. As you're a loyal servant,
And a woman, breathe no word about my purposes.

Exit NURSE.

CHORUS: The people of Athens, sons of Erechtheus,
    have enjoyed their prosperity
Since ancient times. Children of blessed gods,
They grew from holy soil unscorched by invasion.
Among the glories of knowledge their souls are pastured;
They walk always with grace under the sparkling sky.
There long ago, they say, was born golden-haired Harmony,
Created by the nine virgin Muses of Pieria.

They say that Aphrodite dips her cup
In the clear stream of the lovely Cephisus;
It is she who breathes over the land the breath
Of gentle honey-laden winds; her flowing locks
She crowns with a diadem of sweet-scented roses,

And sends the Loves to be enthroned beside Knowledge,
And with her to create excellence in every art.

Then how will such a city,
Watered by sacred rivers,
A country giving protection to its friends –
How will Athens welcome
You, the child-killer
Whose presence is pollution?
Contemplate the blow struck at a child,
Weigh the blood you take upon you.
Medea, by your knees,
By every pledge or appeal we beseech you,
Do not slaughter your children!

Where will you find hardness of purpose?
How will you build resolution in hand or heart
To face horror without flinching?
When the moment comes, and you look at them –
The moment for you to assume the role of murderess –
How will you do it?
When your sons kneel to you for pity,
Will you stain your fingers with their blood?
Your heart will melt; you will know you cannot.

Enter JASON *from the palace. Two maids come from the house to attend Medea.*

JASON: You sent for me: I have come. Although you hate me, I
    Am ready to listen. You have some new request; what is it?
MEDEA: Jason, I ask you to forgive the things I said.
    You must bear with my violent temper; you and I
    Share many memories of love. I have been taking
    Myself to task. 'You are a fool,' I've told myself,
    'You're mad, when people try to plan things for the best,
    To be resentful, and pick quarrels with the King
    And with your husband; what he's doing will help us all.

His wife is royal; her sons will be my sons' brothers.
Why not throw off your anger? What is the matter, since
The gods are making kind provision? After all
I have two children still to care for; and I know
We came as exiles, and our friends are few enough.'
When I considered this, I saw my foolishness;
I saw how useless anger was. So now I welcome
What you have done; I think you are wise to gain for us
This new alliance, and the folly was all mine.
I should have helped you in your plans, made it my pleasure
To get ready your marriage-bed, attend your bride.
But we women – I won't say we are bad by nature,
But we are what we are. You, Jason, should not copy
Our bad example, or match yourself with us, showing
Folly for folly. I give in; I was wrong just now,
I admit. But I have thought more wisely of it since.
Children, children! Are you indoors? Come out here.

> [*The* CHILDREN *come out. Their* TUTOR *follows.*]

Children,
Greet your father, as I do, and put your arms round him.
Forget our quarrel, and love him as your mother does.
We have made friends; we are not angry any more.
There, children; take his hand.

> [*She turns away in a sudden flood of weeping.*]

Forgive me; I recalled
What pain the future hides from us.

> [*After embracing Jason the* CHILDREN *go back to Medea.*]

Oh children! Will you
All your lives long, stretch out your hands to me like this?
Oh, my tormented heart is full of tears and terrors.
After so long, I have ended my quarrel with your father;
And now, see! I have drenched this young face with my tears.
CHORUS: I too feel fresh tears fill my eyes. May the course
    of evil
  Be checked now, go no further!

JASON: I am pleased, Medea,
   That you have changed your mind; though indeed I do not
      blame
   Your first resentment. Only naturally a woman
   Is angry when her husband marries a second wife.
   You have had wiser thoughts; and though it has taken time,
   You have recognized the right decision. This is the act
   Of a sensible woman. As for you, my boys, your father
   Has taken careful thought, and, with the help of the gods,
   Ensured a good life for you. Why, in time, I'm sure,
   You with your brothers will be leading men in Corinth.
   Only grow big and strong. Your father, and those gods
   Who are his friends, have all the rest under control.
   I want to see you, when you're strong, full-grown young
      men,
   Tread down my enemies.
               [*Again* MEDEA *breaks down and weeps.*]
                        What's this? Why these floods of tears?
   Why are you pale? Did you not like what I was saying?
   Why do you turn away?
MEDEA: It is nothing. I was thinking
   About these children.
JASON: I'll provide for them. Cheer up.
MEDEA: I will. It is not that I mean to doubt your word.
   But women – are women; tears come naturally to us.
JASON: Why do you grieve so over the children?
MEDEA: I'm their mother.
   When you just now prayed for them to live long, I wondered
   Whether it would be so; and grief came over me.
   But I've said only part of what I had to say;
   Here is the other thing. Since Creon has resolved
   To send me out of Corinth, I fully recognize
   That for me too this course is best. If I lived here
   I should become a trouble both to you and him.
   People believe I bear a grudge against you all.

So I must go. But the boys – I would like *them* to be
Brought up in your care. Beg Creon to let them stay.
JASON: I don't know if I can persuade him; but I'll try.
MEDEA: Then – get your wife to ask her father to let them
stay.
JASON: Why, certainly; I'm pretty sure she'll win him over.
MEDEA: She will, if she's like other women. But I too
Can help in this. I'll send a present to your wife –
The loveliest things to be found anywhere on earth.
The boys shall take them. – One of you maids, go quickly,
bring
The dress and golden coronet. – They will multiply
Her happiness many times, when she can call her own
A royal, noble husband, and these treasures, which
My father's father the Sun bequeathed to his descendants.
[*A slave has brought a casket, which* MEDEA *now hands to her sons.*]
Boys, hold these gifts. Now carry them to the happy bride,
The princess royal; give them into her own hands.
Go! She will find them all that such a gift should be.
JASON: But why deprive yourself of such things, foolish
woman?
Do you think a royal palace is in want of dresses?
Or gold, do you suppose? Keep them, don't give them away.
If my wife values me at all she will yield to *me*
More than to costly presents, I am sure of that.
MEDEA: Don't stop me. Gifts, they say, persuade even the
gods;
With mortals, gold outweighs a thousand arguments.
The day is hers; from now on *her* prosperity
Will rise to new heights. She is royal and young. To buy
My sons from exile I would give life, not just gold.
Come, children, go both of you into this rich palace;
Kneel down and beg your father's new wife, and my mistress,
That you may not be banished. And above all, see
That she receives my present into her own hands.

46

Go quickly; be successful, and bring good news back,
That what your mother longs for has been granted you.
   Exit JASON *followed by the* CHILDREN *and the* TUTOR.
CHORUS:
> Now I have no more hope,
> No more hope that the children can live;
> They are walking to murder at this moment.
> The bride will receive the golden coronet,
> Receive her merciless destroyer;
> With her own hands she will carefully fit
> The adornment of death round her golden hair.
>
> She cannot resist such loveliness, such heavenly gleaming;
> She will enfold herself
> In the dress and the wreath of wrought gold,
> Preparing her bridal beauty
> To enter a new home – among the dead.
> So fatal is the snare she will fall into,
> So inevitable the death that awaits her;
> From its cruelty there is no escape.
>
> And you, unhappy Jason, ill-starred in marriage,
> You, son-in-law of kings:
> Little you know that the favour you ask
> Will seal your sons' destruction
> And fasten on your wife a hideous fate.
> O wretched Jason!
> So sure of destiny, and so ignorant!
>
> Your sorrow next I weep for, pitiable mother;
> You, for jealousy of your marriage-bed,
> Will slaughter your children;
> Since, disregarding right and loyalty,
> Your husband has abandoned you
> And lives with another wife.

47

The TUTOR *returns from the palace with the two* CHILDREN.

TUTOR: Mistress! These two boys are reprieved from banishment.

The princess took your gifts from them with her own hand,
And was delighted. They have no enemies in the palace.

[MEDEA *is silent.*]

Well, bless my soul!

Isn't that good news? Why do you stand there thunderstruck?

MEAEA [*to herself*]: How cruel, how cruel!

TUTOR: That's out of tune with the news I brought.

MEDEA: How cruel life is!

TUTOR: Have I, without knowing it,
Told something dreadful, then? I thought my news was good.

MEDEA: Your news is what it is. I am not blaming you.

TUTOR: Then why stand staring at the ground, with streaming
eyes?

MEDEA: Strong reason forces me to weep, old friend. The gods,
And my own evil-hearted plots, have led to this.

TUTOR: Take heart, mistress; in time your sons will bring you
home.

MEDEA: Before then, I have others to send home.   Oh, gods!

She weeps.

TUTOR: You're not the only mother parted from her sons.
We are all mortal; you must not bear grief so hard.

MEDEA: Yes, friend. I'll follow your advice. Now go indoors
And get things ready for them, as on other days.

[*Exit* TUTOR. *The* CHILDREN *come to Medea.*]

O children, children! You have a city, and a home;
And when we have parted, there you both will stay for ever,
You motherless, I miserable. And I must go
To exile in another land, before I have had
My joy of you, before I have seen you growing up,
Becoming prosperous. I shall never see your brides,
Adorn your bridal beds, and hold the torches high.

48

My misery is my own heart, which will not relent.
All was for nothing, then – these years of rearing you,
My care, my aching weariness, and the wild pains
When you were born. Oh, yes, I once built many hopes
On you; imagined, pitifully, that you would care
For my old age, and would yourselves wrap my dead body
For burial. How people would envy me my sons!
That sweet, sad thought has faded now. Parted from you,
My life will be all pain and anguish. You will not
Look at your mother any more with these dear eyes.
You will have moved into a different sphere of life.

Dear sons, why are you staring at me so? You smile
At me – your last smile: why?
[*She weeps. The* CHILDREN *go from her a little, and she turns to
the Chorus.*]
                                        Oh, what am I to do?
Women, my courage is all gone. Their young, bright faces ·
I can't do it. I'll think no more of it. I'll take them
Away from Corinth. Why should I hurt *them*, to make
Their father suffer, when I shall suffer twice as much
Myself? I won't do it. I won't think of it again.

What is the matter with me? Are my enemies
To laugh at me? Am I to let them off scot free?
I must steel myself to it. What a coward I am,
Even tempting my own resolution with soft talk.
Boys, go indoors.
[*The* CHILDREN *go to the door, but stay there watching her.*]
                              If there is any here who finds it
Not lawful to be present at my sacrifice,
Let him see to it. My hand shall not weaken.

Oh, my heart, don't, don't do it! Oh, miserable heart,
Let them be! Spare your children! We'll all live together

Safely in Athens; and they will make you happy. . . . No!
No! No! By all the fiends of hate in hell's depths, no!
I'll not leave sons of mine to be the victims of
My enemies' rage. In any case there is no escape,
The thing's done now. Yes, now – the golden coronet
Is on her head, the royal bride is in her dress,
Dying, I know it. So, since I have a sad road
To travel, and send these boys on a still sadder road,
I'll speak to them. Come, children; give me your hand, dear
    son;
Yours too. Now we must say goodbye. Oh, darling hand,
And darling mouth; your noble, childlike face and body!
Dear sons, my blessing on you both – but there, not here!
All blessing here your father has destroyed. How sweet
To hold you! And children's skin is soft, and their breath
    pure.
Go! Go away! I can't look at you any longer;
My pain is more than I can bear.

> [*The* CHILDREN *go indoors.*]
>   I understand

The horror of what I am going to do; but anger,
The spring of all life's horror, masters my resolve.

> MEDEA *goes to stand looking towards the palace.*

CHORUS:

> I have often engaged in arguments,
> And become more subtle, and perhaps more heated,
> Than is suitable for women;
> Though in fact women too have intelligence,
> Which forms part of our nature and instructs us –
> Not all of us, I admit; but a certain few
> You might perhaps find, in a large number of women –
> A few not incapable of reflection;
>
> And this is my opinion: those men or women
> Who never had children of their own at all

50

Enjoy the advantage in good fortune
Over those who are parents. Childless people
Have no means of knowing whether children are
A blessing or a burden; but being without them
They live exempt from many troubles.

While those who have growing up in their homes
The sweet gift of children I see always
Burdened and worn with incessant worry,
First, how to rear them in health and safety,
And bequeath them, in time, enough to live on;
And then this further anxiety:
They can never know whether all their toil
Is spent for worthy or worthless children.

And beyond the common ills that attend
All human life there is one still worse:
Suppose at last they are pretty well off,
Their children have grown up, and, what's more,
Are kind and honest: then what happens?
A throw of chance – and there goes Death
Bearing off your child into the unknown.

Then why should mortals thank the gods,
Who add to their load, already grievous,
This one more grief, for their children's sake,
Most grievous of all?

MEDEA: Friends, I have long been waiting for a message from
the palace.
What is to happen next? I see a slave of Jason's
Coming, gasping for breath. He must bring fearful news.

Enter a MESSENGER.

MESSENGER: Medea! Get away, escape! Oh, what a thing
to do!
What an unholy, horrible thing! Take ship, or chariot,
Any means you can, but escape!

MEDEA: Why should I escape?

MESSENGER: She's dead – the princess, and her father Creon too,
  They're both dead, by your poisons.

MEDEA: Your news is excellent.
  I count you from today my friend and benefactor.

MESSENGER: What? Are you sane, or raving mad? When you've committed
  This hideous crime against the royal house, you're glad
  At hearing of it? Do you not tremble at such things?

MEDEA: I could make suitable reply to that, my friend.
  But take your time now; tell me, how did they die? You'll give
  Me double pleasure if their death was horrible.

MESSENGER: When your two little boys came hand in hand, and entered
  The palace with their father, where the wedding was,
  We servants were delighted. We had all felt sorry
  To hear how you'd been treated; and now the word went round
  From one to another, that you and Jason had made it up.
  So we were glad to see the boys; one kissed their hand,
  Another their fair hair. Myself, I was so pleased,
  I followed with them to the princess's room. Our mistress –
  The one we now call mistress in your place – before
  She saw your pair of boys coming, had eyes only
  For Jason; but seeing them she dropped her eyes, and turned
  Her lovely cheek away, upset that they should come
  Into her room. Your husband then began to soothe
  Her sulkiness, her girlish temper. 'You must not,'
  He said, 'be unfriendly to our friends. Turn your head round,
  And give up feeling angry. Those your husband loves
  You must love too. Now take these gifts,' he said, 'and ask
  Your father to revoke their exile for my sake.'

So, when she saw those lovely things, she was won over,
And agreed to all that Jason asked. At once, before
He and your sons were well out of the house, she took
The embroidered gown and put it round her. Then she placed
Over her curls the golden coronet, and began
To arrange her hair in a bright mirror, smiling at
Her lifeless form reflected there. Then she stood up,
And to and fro stepped daintily about the room
On white bare feet, and many times she would twist back
To see how the dress fell in clear folds to the heel.

Then suddenly we saw a frightening thing. She changed
Colour; she staggered sideways, shook in every limb.
She was just able to collapse on to a chair,
Or she would have fallen flat. Then one of her attendants,
An old woman, thinking that perhaps the anger of Pan
Or some other god had struck her, chanted the cry of worship.
But then she saw, oozing from the girl's lips, white froth;
The pupils of her eyes were twisted out of sight;
The blood was drained from all her skin. The old woman knew
Her mistake, and changed her chant to a despairing howl.
One maid ran off quickly to fetch the King, another
To look for Jason and tell him what was happening
To his young bride; the whole palace was filled with a clatter
Of people running here and there.

                                        All this took place
In a few moments, perhaps while a fast runner might run
A hundred yards; and she lay speechless, with eyes closed.
Then she came to, poor girl, and gave a frightful scream,
As two torments made war on her together: first
The golden coronet round her head discharged a stream
Of unnatural devouring fire: while the fine dress

Your children gave her – poor miserable girl! – the stuff
Was eating her clear flesh. She leapt up from her chair,
On fire, and ran, shaking her head and her long hair
This way and that, trying to shake off the coronet.
The ring of gold was fitted close and would not move;
The more she shook her head the fiercer the flame burned.
At last, exhausted by agony, she fell to the ground;
Save to her father, she was unrecognizable.
Her eyes, her face, were one grotesque disfigurement;
Down from her head dripped blood mingled with flame; her
    flesh,
Attacked by the invisible fangs of poison, melted
From the bare bone, like gum-drops from a pine-tree's
    bark –
A ghastly sight. Not one among us dared to touch
Her body. What we'd seen was lesson enough for us.

But suddenly her father came into the room.
He did not understand, poor man, what kind of death
Had struck his child. He threw himself down at her side,
And sobbed aloud, and kissed her, and took her in his
    arms,
And cried, 'Poor darling child, what god destroyed your life
So cruelly? Who robs me of my only child,
Old as I am, and near my grave? Oh, let me die
With you, my daughter!' Soon he ceased his tears and cries,
And tried to lift his aged body upright; and then,
As ivy sticks to laurel-branches, so he stuck
Fast to the dress. A ghastly wrestling then began;
He struggled to raise up his knee, she tugged him down.
If he used force, he tore the old flesh off his bones.
At length the King gave up his pitiful attempts;
Weakened with pain, he yielded, and gasped out his life.
Now, joined in death, daughter and father – such a sight
As tears were made for – they lie there.

To you, Medea,
I have no more to say. You will yourself know best
How to evade reprisal. As for human life,
It is a shadow, as I have long believed. And this
I say without hesitation: those whom most would call
Intelligent, the propounders of wise theories –
Their folly is of all men's the most culpable.
Happiness is a thing no man possesses. Fortune
May come now to one man, now to another, as
Prosperity increases; happiness never.

Exit MESSENGER.

CHORUS: Today we see the will of Heaven, blow after blow,
Bring down on Jason justice and calamity.

MEDEA: Friends, now my course is clear: as quickly as
    possible
To kill the children and then fly from Corinth; not
Delay and so consign them to another hand
To murder with a better will. For they must die,
In any case; and since they must, then I who gave
Them birth will kill them. Arm yourself, my heart: the
    thing
That you must do is fearful, yet inevitable.
Why wait, then? My accursed hand, come, take the sword;
Take it, and forward to your frontier of despair.
No cowardice, no tender memories; forget
That you once loved them, that of your body they were born.
For one short day forget your children; afterwards
Weep: though you kill them, they were your beloved sons.
Life has been cruel to me.

MEDEA *goes into the house.*

CHORUS: Earth, awake! Bright arrows of the Sun,
Look! Look down on the accursed woman
Before she lifts up a murderous hand
To pollute it with her children's blood!
For they are of your own golden race;

55

And for mortals to spill blood that grew
In the veins of gods is a fearful thing.
Heaven-born brightness, hold her, stop her,
Purge the palace of her, this pitiable
Bloody-handed fiend of vengeance!

All your care for them lost! Your love
For the babes you bore, all wasted, wasted!
Why did you come from the blue Symplegades
That hold the gate of the barbarous sea?
Why must this rage devour your heart
To spend itself in slaughter of children?
Where kindred blood pollutes the ground
A curse hangs over human lives;
And murder measures the doom that falls
By Heaven's law on the guilty house.

A child's scream is heard from inside the house.

CHORUS: Do you hear? The children are calling for help.
    O cursed, miserable woman!
CHILDREN'S VOICES: Help, help! Mother, let me go!
    Mother, don't kill us!
CHORUS: Shall we go in?
    I am sure we ought to save the children's lives.
CHILDREN'S VOICES: Help, help, for the gods' sake! She
    is killing us!
    We can't escape from her sword!
CHORUS: O miserable mother, to destroy your own increase,
    Murder the babes of your body!
    Stone and iron you are, as you resolved to be.

There was but one in time past,
One woman that I have heard of,
Raised hand against her own children.
It was Ino, sent out of her mind by a god,
When Hera, the wife of Zeus,

56

Drove her from her home to wander over the world.
In her misery she plunged into the sea
Being defiled by the murder of her children;
From the steep cliff's edge she stretched out her foot,
And so ended,
Joined in death with her two sons.

What can be strange or terrible after this?
O bed of women, full of passion and pain,
What wickedness, what sorrow you have caused on the
     earth!

                    Enter JASON, *running and breathless.*

JASON: You women standing round the door there! Is Medea
     Still in the house? – vile murderess! – or has she gone
     And escaped? I swear she must either hide in the deep earth
     Or soar on wings into the sky's abyss, to escape
     My vengeance for the royal house. – She has killed the King
     And the princess! Does she expect to go unpunished?

     Well, I am less concerned with her than with the children.
     Those who have suffered at her hands will make her suffer;
     I've come to save my sons, before Creon's family
     Murder them in revenge for this unspeakable
     Crime of their mother's.

CHORUS: Jason, you have yet to learn
     How great your trouble is; or you would not have spoken so.

JASON: What trouble? Is Medea trying to kill me too?

CHORUS: Your sons are dead. Their mother has killed both
     your sons.

JASON: What? Killed my sons? That word kills me.

CHORUS: They are both dead.

JASON: Where are they? Did she kill them out here, or
     indoors?

CHORUS: Open that door, and see them lying in their blood.

JASON: Slaves, there! Unbar the doors! Open, and let me see

57

Two horrors: my dead sons, and the woman I will kill.

JASON *batters at the doors.* MEDEA *appears above the roof, sitting
in a chariot drawn by dragons, with the bodies of the two children
beside her.*

MEDEA: Jason! Why are you battering at these doors, seeking
The dead children and me who killed them? Stop! Be quiet.
If you have any business with me, say what you wish.
Touch us you cannot, in this chariot which the Sun
Has sent to save us from the hands of enemies.

JASON: You abomination! Of all women most detested
By every god, by me, by the whole human race!
You could endure – a mother! – to lift sword against
Your own little ones; to leave me childless, my life wrecked.
After such murder do you outface both Sun and Earth –
Guilty of gross pollution? May the gods blast your life!
I am sane now; but I was mad before, when I
Brought you from your palace in a land of savages
Into a Greek home – you, a living curse, already
A traitor both to your father and your native land.
The vengeance due for your sins the gods have cast on me.
You had already murdered your brother at his own hearth
When first you stepped on board my lovely Argo's hull.
That was your beginning. Then you became my wife, and
    bore
My children; now, out of mere sexual jealousy,
You murder them! In all Hellas there is not one woman
Who could have done it; yet in preference to them
I married you, chose hatred and murder for my wife –
No woman, but a tiger; a Tuscan Scylla – but more savage.
Ah, what's the use? If I cursed you all day, no remorse
Would touch you, for your heart's proof against feeling. Go!
Out of my sight, polluted fiend, child-murderer!
Leave me to mourn over my destiny: I have lost
My young bride; I have lost the two sons I begot
And brought up; I shall never see them alive again.

MEDEA: I would if necessary have answered at full length
Everything you have said; but Zeus the father of all
Knows well what service I once rendered you, and how
You have repaid me. You were mistaken if you thought
You could dishonour my bed and live a pleasant life
And laugh at me. The princess was wrong too, and so
Was Creon, when he took you for his son-in-law
And thought he could exile me with impunity.
So now, am I a tiger, Scylla? – Hurl at me
What names you please! I've reached your heart; and that is
   right.

JASON: You suffer too; my loss is yours no less.

MEDEA: It is true;
But my pain's a fair price, to take away your smile.

JASON: O children, what a wicked mother Fate gave you!

MEDEA: O sons, your father's treachery cost you your lives.

JASON: It was not my hand that killed my sons.

MEDEA: No, not your hand;
But your insult to me, and your new-wedded wife.

JASON: You thought *that* reason enough to murder them,
   that I
No longer slept with you?

MEDEA: And is that injury
A slight one, do you imagine, to a woman?

JASON: Yes,
To a modest woman; but to you – the whole world lost.

MEDEA: I can stab too: your sons are dead!

JASON: Dead? No! They live –
To haunt your life with vengeance.

MEDEA: Who began this feud?
The gods know.

JASON: Yes – they know the vileness of your heart.

MEDEA: Loathe on! Your bitter voice – how I abhor the
   sound!

JASON: As I loathe yours. Let us make terms and part at once.

MEDEA: Most willingly. What terms? What do you bid me
do?

JASON: Give me my sons for burial and mourning rites.

MEDEA: Oh, no! I will myself convey them to the temple
Of Hera Acraea; there in the holy precinct I
Will bury them with my own hand, to ensure t hat none
Of my enemies shall violate or insult their graves.
And I will ordain an annual feast and sacrifice
To be solemnized for ever by the people of Corinth,
To expiate this impious murder. I myself
Will go to Athens, city of Erechtheus, to make my home
With Aegeus son of Pandion. You, as you deserve,
Shall die an unheroic death, your head shattered
By a timber from the Argo's hull. Thus wretchedly
Your fate shall end the story of your love for me.

JASON: The curse of children's blood be on you!
Avenging Justice blast your being!

MEDEA: What god will hear your imprecation,
Oath-breaker, guest-deceiver, liar?

JASON: Unclean, abhorrent child-destroyer!

MEDEA: Go home: your wife waits to be buried.

JASON: I go – a father once; now childless.

MEDEA: You grieve too soon. Old age is coming.

JASON: Children, how dear you were!

MEDEA: To their mother; not to you.

JASON: Dear – and you murdered them?

MEDEA: Yes, Jason, to break your heart.

JASON: I long to fold them in my arms;
To kiss their lips would comfort me.

MEDEA: *Now* you have loving words, now kisses for them:
Then you disowned them, sent them into exile.

JASON: For God's sake, let me touch their gentle flesh.

MEDEA: You shall not. It is waste of breath to ask.

JASON:
Zeus, do you hear how I am mocked,

Rejected, by this savage beast
Polluted with her children's blood?

But now, as time and strength permit,
I will lament this grievous day,
And call the gods to witness, how
You killed my sons, and now refuse
To let me touch or bury them.
Would God I had not bred them,
Or ever lived to see
Them dead, you their destroyer!

During this speech the chariot has moved out of sight.

CHORUS: Many are the Fates which Zeus in Olympus dispenses;
Many matters the gods bring to surprising ends.
The things we thought would happen do not happen;
The unexpected God makes possible;
And such is the conclusion of this story.

HECABE

*

Characters:

GHOST OF POLYDORUS, *son of Priam and Hecabe*
HECABE, *formerly Queen of Troy*
POLYXENA, *her daughter*
ODYSSEUS, *a Greek commander*
TALTHYBIUS, *Herald of the Greek army*
AGAMEMNON, *Commander-in-Chief of the Greek army*
POLYMESTOR, *King of Thrace*
AN OLD WOMAN *attending Hecabe*
CHORUS *of Trojan Women held prisoners by Agamemnon*

*

*The scene is before Agamemnon's tent, near the shore of the Thracian
   Peninsula (on the opposite side of the Strait from Troy), where the
   Greek army is encamped. The* GHOST OF POLYDORUS
   appears above Agamemnon's tent.

POLYDORUS: From sombre caverns of the secret earth, from
      gates
   Of darkness where, far from the company of gods,
   Hades governs his colony – from the dead I come.
   I am Polydorus, son of Hecabe and King Priam.
   My father, when Troy was ringed round with Hellene
      spears,
   Fearing the city's capture, smuggled me away
   To Thrace, to the palace of his old friend Polymestor,
   Who farms the fertile plain of this peninsula
   And rules over a race of horsemen with his sword.
   With me my father sent a secret store of gold,
   So that, if ever Troy should fall, there might remain
   Enough to rescue his surviving sons from want.

Of Priam's sons I was the youngest; that was why
He sent me away; I was not old or strong enough
For armour or a sword. So, while the outer wall
Of Troy stood firm, her towers unbroken, and in the field
My brother Hector was victorious, I enjoyed
A happy life there with my father's Thracian friend,
And grew like a young sapling, cared-for, unaware
Of destiny.

        But when Troy fell, and Hector fell,
And Priam's palace lay in dust, and Priam himself,
Grasping the holy altar, fell in his own blood
Before the impious sword of Neoptolemus,
My father's guest-friend Polymestor murdered me,
To get my gold and keep it; and having murdered me
He threw my body into the sea. Now I lie there
Stretched on the shingle, floating in the salty foam,
By racing currents rolled endlessly to and fro,
Unwept, unburied. Now, abandoning my body,
I have come to hover close over the suffering head
Of my dear mother Hecabe. For three days now
I float about her, since they brought her here from Troy.

Meanwhile the Achaeans sit here on the Thracian shore,
Their ships all idle. For, just as the Hellene fleet,
With all the army on board, were dipping oars for home,
Achilles, Peleus' son, appeared above his tomb
And held them back; demanding that Polyxena,
My sister, as a gift of honour for his tomb,
Be sacrificed there. And this will be granted him;
For they all loved him, and will give him what he asks.
Fate leads my sister to her death this very day.
My mother then shall see two bodies of her children,
Mine and my sister's, lying dead before her eyes.
For I have begged the powers below to let me come
Into my mother's hands, and be given burial.

So I shall appear to her; one of her maids will find me
Cast up by the sea; and my poor body will be buried.
That done, I shall have all I wish.

                              I see my mother
Coming from Agamemnon's tent. I'll leave her now.
She has seen my phantom in her dream, and is distressed.
– Oh, mother, mother! After your royal palace – this!
A slave! From highest height to lowest depth! Some god
Saw your old glory, and counterpoised it with this ruin.

Exit the GHOST OF POLYDORUS. *Enter* HECABE *from the tent,*
                    supported by two younger women.

HECABE: Help me, my daughters; hold the old woman up,
   Your fellow-slave now, Trojans; once your queen.
      Now hold my arms and take me,
      Come with me and support me.
   I'm old; I have to lean on this curved stick
   And try to make my slow feet and stiff joints
      Move on a little faster.
   O dazzling light of day, O murk of night,
      Why am I roused and raptured
      With haunting fears and phantoms?
   O holy Earth, mother of dark-winged dreams,
   Take back this frightful vision I have seen!
      I dreamt of Polydorus,
      Sent into Thrace for safety,
   And of my darling girl Polyxena.
   Gods of the lower world, keep my son safe,
      Where in the wintry mountains
      His father's friend protects him!
   He is the only anchor of our house.
      Some new grief looms, fresh weeping
      For eyes tear-drowned already.
   A dread not felt before pounds at my heart.
   Oh, friends, were Helenus or Cassandra here,

65

That their divine foreknowledge
  Might tell me my dream's meaning!
I saw a dappled fawn cruelly dragged
From the protection of my lap, and torn
  By a wolf's fangs, and slaughtered.
  And this fear will not leave me:
Achilles' ghost appeared above his tomb
And claimed a maiden's blood in sacrifice –
  One of us suffering Trojans.
  Then, O you gods, I beg you,
Avert this fate, avert it from my child!

                    Enter the CHORUS.

CHORUS: Hecabe, I have slipped away quickly to find you,
  From Agamemnon's tent, where we have been
  Since we were driven from Troy by the Achaeans
  As their spoils of war,
  Drawn for, and allotted to him as slaves.
  My news will not lighten your suffering;
  To carry such words is a grievous burden,
  And for you they are agony to bear.
  The Achaeans, they say, in full assembly
  Resolved to sacrifice your daughter to Achilles.

  You remember when he appeared
  Standing in golden armour above his tomb
  And checked the sea-going vessels
  When sails were already taut on the rigging
  With this cry: 'Where are you going, you Greeks,
  Abandoning my grave without a gift?'

  Then in the council of Greek spearmen
  Two factions, like wave meeting wave,
  Clashed in a fierce dispute;
  These cried 'Sacrifice!' and those cried 'No!'
  The one who took your part was Agamemnon,

Faithful to his love for the frenzied prophetess;
But the two Athenians, the sons of Theseus,
Though making two different proposals,
Were united in this opinion,
That Achilles' tomb should be crowned with living blood.
It was wrong, they said, to give more consideration
To Cassandra's bed than to Achilles' spear.

And the argument pulled equally both ways,
Till that cunning, honey-tongued quibbler,
That pleaser of the mob, Odysseus, urged them
Not to dishonour the bravest of all the Greeks
For the sake of a slave's throat.
'Shall the dead souls,' he cried,
'Who stand in the presence of Persephone
Say that Greeks forget their debts to Greeks?
That we came away from the plains of Troy
Neglecting those who died there for our country?'

Very soon Odysseus will be coming
To drag your child from your embrace,
Pull hand from hand and take her.
So come, kneel at the altar,
Fall as a suppliant at Agamemnon's knees,
Cry aloud to the gods of heaven
And to gods below the earth.
It may be, prayers can save you
From losing your daughter so cruelly; if not,
You must see her fall bleeding before a tomb,
While from her maiden throat
Over her gold necklace the dark flow gleams.

HECABE: O misery, misery!
What word is left to utter?
What cry, what groan can help?
Wretched, old and wretched;

And slavery is unendurable!
Who will help me now?
I have no child, no city;
My husband gone, all my sons gone!
What way can I turn?
Which of the gods or other powers
Will come to our help?
O women, what a message to bring me,
What news to tell me!
Now there is nothing, nothing left in life.
Come, old as you are, rise to your feet,
You must go to her – Daughter, Polyxena!
Come out, come out here to your unhappy mother!
Hear what I have to tell you, child –
What a terrible, terrible word they have brought me –
About your life.

Enter POLYXENA.

POLYXENA: Mother, mother, why are you crying?
Why did you call me so loudly
As if you were scaring a bird from a bush?

HECABE: Oh, my child!

POLYXENA: What is the matter? It must be something
dreadful.

HECABE: Oh, child! Your life, your life!

POLYXENA: Speak out, mother, don't keep it hidden.
I am afraid of what your crying may mean –
I am afraid.

HECABE: O darling child, how we suffer!

POLYXENA: What are you telling me?

HECABE: The Greeks have resolved with one voice
To kill you at the tomb of the son of Peleus.

POLYXENA: Mother, how can you say so horrible a thing?
Tell me plainly, mother, tell me.

HECABE: I am telling you, child, the wicked truth that I
heard:

68

The Argives have passed a resolution to take your life.

POLYXENA: Poor mother! Poor, unhappy mother,
How you have suffered!
What frightful, unspeakable outrage
Some malignant Power has invented
To hurl against your head!
You will not have a daughter any more;
I shall not share with you the wretchedness of slavery,
Nor care for your old age.
You shall see me taken from you
Like a mountain cub torn from its dam;
I shall go to the deep darkness of Hades,
And there among the dead I shall lie with my throat cut.
For your unhappiness, mother,
I weep and mourn with all my heart;
But, for my own life,
Which is nothing now but shame and misery,
I do not weep. I am to die,
And that is the happier lot.

ODYSSEUS *approaches*.

CHORUS: Look, Hecabe!
I see Odysseus hurrying here to speak with you.

ODYSSEUS: Madam, I think you know the Greek army's
decision
Reached by a vote in council; none the less I'll tell you.
They have resolved to sacrifice Polyxena
Your daughter at the high mound of Achilles' tomb.
They have appointed me to come and bring her there;
As priest and overseer of this sacrifice
Achilles' son is chosen. So, you know your part.
Do not be dragged from her by force, or match your strength
With mine. Know that you have none, that your day has
come.
When things are worst, it's still wise to be rational.

HECABE: Truly a mighty struggle lies before me now;

One loud with groans and dark with tears. I should have
   died
Before; I did not die, but Zeus preserved me alive
To see each new pain, each disaster, crowned with worse.
Yet, if a slave may address to a free man such questions
As should not vex or sting the heart, please listen now;
And when I have asked, it is for me to hear you speak.

ODYSSEUS: You are free to ask me; time at least I do not
   grudge.

HECABE: You came once as a spy to Troy – do you remember? –
   Disguised in filthy wrappings, with your eyes and face
   Battered, and trickling blood over your beard?

ODYSSEUS: I do.

HECABE: And Helen recognized you, and told no one but me.

ODYSSEUS: Yes; that day's danger made a deep impression
   on me.

HECABE: You clasped my knees then as a humble suppliant.

ODYSSEUS: Clung to your dress as if my hand was rooted
   there.

HECABE: That day you were my slave. What were your words
   to me?

ODYSSEUS: I invented twenty arguments to save my life.

HECABE: *I* saved you, did I not? – and sent you back from
   Troy.

ODYSSEUS: You did indeed; and here I am alive today.

HECABE: Yet now you scheme these cowardly plots against
   me – you
   Who by your own confession owe me your own life –
   Repaying good with the worst evil in your power!
   You are a low and loathsome breed, all you who grasp
   At popular honours! who without a thought betray
   Your friends, for one phrase that will gratify a mob!
   Let me not know you! Your Greeks – did they think, per-
   haps,
   They had found a neat excuse for passing their decree

To shed this child's blood? What was it persuaded them
To spurn the more appropriate offering of a bull,
And signalize this grave with human sacrifice?
Was it their sense of duty? Or did Achilles want
A life in payment for his life? How just, to choose
This girl! What injury has my daughter done to him?
He should have claimed Helen as victim for his tomb;
She killed him, since it was for her he came to Troy.
If you must pick for death one of your prisoners
Supreme in beauty, why look among us? Helen
Outshines us all – and injured him, and you, far more.
That answers your pretence of justice; but now hear
What gratitude demands from you, in answer to
My pleading. As you admit, you clasped my hand, and knelt
Before me, and touched my cheek. I kneel to you, and touch
    Your hand, your cheek. I beg in turn what you begged
    then.
I implore you, do not tear my child from me, do not
Kill her. There is enough death. In her lies my joy,
In her I forget troubles, and find comfort for
All I have lost. She is my city now; my nurse,
My staff, my guide. The strong ought not to use their
    strength
To do what is not right; when they are fortunate
They should not think Fortune will always favour them.
I once was fortunate, and now I am so no more;
One day has taken happiness, wealth, everything.
Then be my friend. Let awe, and pity, move your heart.
Go to the Achaean army; talk them round; tell them
What odium will fasten on you, if you kill
Women whom first you did not kill, but pitied, when
You dragged them from the altars. In your country's law
Killing is killing – there is no distinction made
Of slave and free man. Speak to them; your reputation

71

Will sway them, even with doubtful arguments. A word
Has double power, coming from one whom men respect.

CHORUS: No human heart could be so hardened, that your pleas
And pitiful lamentations would not move to tears.

ODYSSEUS: Listen, Hecabe, and learn; and do not in your anger
Take for an enemy one who gives you good advice.
You saved my life; and I am ready to save yours –
I give my word. But I will not go back on what
I said in open council, that, now Troy is taken,
The first man of our army, Achilles, must be given
Your daughter, as the victim he demands of us.
Most cities suffer from this very thing, that men
Who are brave and patriotic reap no more reward
Than shirkers. We Greeks honour above all other men
Achilles, who gave his life for Hellas. While he lived
We were his friends; if, when he dies, we are friends no longer,
Is it not shameful? Just suppose, now, that once more
We had to mobilize and fight our enemies:
A man would ask himself, 'Shall I join up and fight?
Or stay safe here at home, seeing that those who are killed
Receive no special honour?' As far as I'm concerned,
While I'm alive, I'm satisfied with very little,
Enough for daily needs; but, when I'm dead, I want
My tomb to be a thing men gaze at reverently.
That is a gift which lasts. And if you think, Hecabe,
That what you suffer is pitiful, let me tell you this:
We have at home old women no less miserable
Than you, and old men too, and young wives who have lost
Heroic husbands, buried here in Trojan dust.
You must endure this. As for us, if we are wrong
In honouring our valiant dead, we will admit
The charge of folly. And you foreigners, continue

72

Treating your friends as no friends, and dishonouring
Those who died nobly; so that Hellas may grow great,
While you will reap the fruits of your ingratitude.

CHORUS: O gods! How wretched is the condition of a slave,
Forced to endure the wickedness of conquerors!

HECABE: Oh, daughter! All my pleading for your life is lost,
Gone, scattered to the winds. Perhaps your words will have
More power than mine. Speak to him. Let your voice use all
The sweetness of the nightingale, to win your life.
Stir him to pity. Fall and clasp his knees. He too
Has children – speak of them; he may yet pity you.

POLYXENA: I see you hiding your right hand under your cloak,
Odysseus, and turning your head away, in case
I try to touch your beard; but set your mind at rest.
You need fear no embarrassing appeal from me.
I'll come with you – because I must, but also because
To die is what I wish. If it were not, I should
Be known for a coward, prizing life beyond its worth.
For what is life worth to me? When my life began
My father ruled all Phrygia. Lapped in splendid hopes
I was brought up a bride for princes; rival thrones
And palaces contended, which should call me Queen.
Matrons of Troy bowed to me as their mistress; girls
Looked at me enviously. I was a god, in all
Except mortality. Now I am a slave. That name
Alone, being new to me, makes me in love with death.
Then, chance might give me a harsh-minded master, who,
Having paid money for me, would send me to his kitchen –
Sister of Hector and many others royally born –
To make bread, sweep the house, stand weaving at the loom:
Day after day of bitterness! And some bought slave
Would claim my bed, soiling what kings once sued to have.
Never! I will yield up this daylight from free eyes;
Hades shall have my body. Lead on; take your part,
Odysseus, in my death. I see the future clearly:

73

Neither hope nor imagination promises
A good life, ever. Mother, say nothing, do nothing
To stop me, but consent that I must die, before
Dishonour too be offered, which we have not deserved.
One unaccustomed to the taste of misery
Bears it, but suffers as his neck accepts the yoke.
For such a one there is more happiness in dying
Than living. A sordid life is bitterness and gall.

CHORUS: The stamp of royal birth is an unmistakable
   Miracle; and when those who bear a noble name
   Are worthy of it, the miracle is greater still.

HECABE: My daughter, you have spoken nobly; but the price
   Of nobleness is heavy. [To Odysseus] If Achilles must
   Be satisfied, and you Greeks must avoid reproach,
   Then take *me* to his tomb, stab *me* – why hesitate?
   Don't kill my daughter; it was I gave Paris birth,
   Who shot Achilles with his bow, and caused his death.

ODYSSEUS: Achilles asked for your daughter, Hecabe, not you.

HECABE: Then kill me with her; so both Earth, and the dead
   soul
   Who claims this blood-offering, shall gain a double draught.

ODYSSEUS: I wish we did not owe one death. It would be
   wrong
   To add another, when your daughter's will suffice.

HECABE: I must, I will die with her.

ODYSSEUS: I was not aware
   That I must take your orders.

HECABE: I will cling to her
   Like ivy to the oak.

ODYSSEUS: Not if you take the advice
   Of one who is wiser.

HECABE: I will never let her go.

ODYSSEUS: Be sure that I will not go back and leave her here.

POLYXENA: Mother, let me persuade you. – Sir, be tolerant;
   My mother has good reason for her passionate words. –

74

Dear mother, force is on his side; don't fight with him.
Do you want to be thrown prostrate on the ground, wounded,
Dragged, hustled, pushed? dishonour done to your old age
By a young man? That is how he will treat you. So,
Don't struggle. It is not worthy of you. Darling mother,
Give me your dear hand; let your cheek rest close to mine.
This is the last time I shall ever see the sun –
So round, so glorious. This is my last good-bye to you,
My own dear mother. Now I am going into the dark.

HECABE: And I in the sun's light, my child, shall live a slave.

POLYXENA: No wedding-song, no husband's love, no hopes
fulfilled.

HECABE: Poor child, how pitiful! And I – how miserable!

POLYXENA: I shall be parted from you, lying in my tomb.

HECABE: O gods, what shall I do? Where is my life to end?

POLYXENA: Born free, of a free father, I shall die a slave.

HECABE: And all my children, all are taken away.

POLYXENA: What message
Shall I give Hector and my father Priam from you?

HECABE: Tell him, of all women I am the most miserable.

POLYXENA: Dear breast, where once you nourished and
protected me!

HECABE: Dear child, condemned by Fate to die in your fresh
youth!

POLYXENA: Farewell; and bid Cassandra farewell too, from
me.

HECABE: Others *fare well*: for me that word is meaningless.

POLYXENA: My brother Polydorus too, far off in Thrace.

HECABE: If he still lives. Can even one joy be left to me?

POLYXENA: He lives, mother; and when you die he'll close
your eyes.

HECABE: Sorrow and suffering have destroyed me. I am dead.

POLYXENA: Take me, Odysseus. Wrap my cloak over my
head.

While death is still before me, my heart melts to hear

My mother weep; and her heart melts to see my tears.
O light! I still can say that word; but all the light
That now belongs to me is what remains between
This moment and the sword beside Achilles' tomb.

        Exeunt ODYSSEUS *and* POLYXENA.

HECABE: Hold me, I am fainting. All my strength is gone.
   Daughter,
  Reach out your hand and touch me. Where's your hand?
   Don't go,
  Don't leave me now, my only child! Polyxena!

        HECABE *collapses on the ground.*

CHORUS:
    Winds, winds of the sea,
    Who carry sea-going vessels
    Rapidly over the moving swell,
    To what place will you bring me?
    Whose house shall I enter
    As his newly-acquired possession?
    Shall I reach some harbour-town in Peloponnese?
    Or in Thessaly, whose farm-land, they say,
    Is made fertile by Apidanus,
    Father of crystal waters?

    Or, as our ship travels the salt sea-roads
    Among the islands, shall I find my sad home
    Where the first palm was planted,
    And the first laurel spread holy boughs
    To shelter Leto in her labour
    And grace the birth of Zeus's children?
    Shall I join with girls of Delos
    In praising the goddess of the golden frontlet,
    Artemis armed with her bow?

    Perhaps I shall come to live in Athene's city,
    And there on the saffron robe of Pallas,

Weaving bright threads in a flowery pattern,
Yoke the horses to her glorious chariot;
Or depict the race of raging Titans
Quelled by Zeus, son of Cronos,
With the flame of his lightning.

Oh, my children, my children!
My poor father! My country!
Every house a smouldering ruin,
Every soul a prisoner,
Spoils of war for the men of Argos!
And I, in a foreign country,
Bearing the name of slave,
Transplanted far from Asia
Into a European home,
Shall live the life of the dead in Hades.

Enter TALTHYBIUS; *at the same time an* OLD TROJAN
WOMAN *comes from the tent and goes to Hecabe.*

TALTHYBIUS: Tell me, young women, where should I find
Hecabe,
The former queen of Troy?

CHORUS: Close by you, Talthybius,
She lies stretched on the ground, her dress veiling her
face.

TALTHYBIUS: O Zeus! What is the truth? Do you behold
men's lives?
Or is all our belief in gods a myth, a lie
Foolishly cherished, while blind hazard rules the world?
Is this Hecabe, queen of golden Phrygia?
Was this the wife of Priam, renowned for wealth and power?
Now where is Troy? Conquered in war, annihilated;
And she, an aged, childless slave-woman who lies
Prostrate, soiling her pitiful old head with dust.
Well, well! I'm an old man; but I would pray for death
Sooner than come to anything like this. – Hecabe!

77

Get up; stand up, now; raise your white head from the
ground.

HECABE: Who is it will not let my body lie at peace?
I am in great grief; why disturb me? Who are you?

TALTHYBIUS: I am Talthybius, herald of the Greek army.
Agamemnon, lady, sent me here; I've come for you.

HECABE: Friend! Have the Greeks resolved to sacrifice me
too?
You have come to fetch me to the altar? You are welcome!
Let's lose no time; show me the way, Talthybius.

TALTHYBIUS: Your daughter, Hecabe, is dead; and by com-
mand
Of the two sons of Atreus and the Greek army
I have come now to fetch you for her burial rites.

HECABE: I hoped you had come to bring me there to die;
instead
You tell me this – O child, they took you from your mother,
And killed you. And I am left alone to weep for you.
– How did you kill her? Was it honourably done?
Or did you spare no horror, since your victim was
An enemy? Tell me fully; I can bear it all.

TALTHYBIUS: You ask me, lady, to incur a double share
Of tears, in pity for your daughter. When she died
I wept; and I shall weep again in telling of it.
There in front of the grave stood the whole multitude
Of the Achaean army, to see the sacrifice.
Achilles' son led Polyxena by the hand
Up to the summit of the mound. I stood close by.
Behind us, a picked group of young Achaeans stood
Ready to hold her if she struggled to escape.
A cup of pure gold had been placed there, full of wine
For a libation to Achilles' ghost. His son
Lifted the cup, and told me to command silence
Throughout the assembled army. I stood up and called,
'Silence, Achaeans; let neither voice nor sound be heard

78

In the whole army.' I had them hushed and motionless.
Then he spoke: 'O my father, Peleus' son, receive
From me this soothing wine that summons parted souls.
Then come, drink this maid's dark untainted blood, which I
And the whole army offer you; and look on us
With favour, granting that we may unmoor our ships,
And with a prosperous voyage come safe to our own land.'
Such were his words; and all prayed with him. Then he
    grasped
His sword by the gold hilt, drew it from the sheath, and
    signed
To the young men appointed, to take hold of her.
Polyxena saw; and this is what she said: 'You Greeks,
Who laid my city in ruins, I die willingly.
Let no one lay hands on me; I will give my neck
Steadfastly to the sword. So, in the name of God,
Let me stand free, and kill me; then I shall die free.
Since I am royal, to be called slave among the dead
Would be dishonour.' The whole army roared consent;
And Agamemnon told the youths to set her free.
When she heard this, she took hold of her dress, and tore it
From shoulder-knot to waist, and showed her breasts, and
    all
Her body to the navel, like the loveliest
Of statues. Then she knelt down on one knee, and spoke
The most heroic words of all: 'Son of Achilles,
Here is my breast, if that is where you wish to strike;
Or if my throat, my neck is ready here; strike home.'
He with his sword – torn between pity and resolve –
Cut through the channels of her breath. A spring of blood
Gushed forth; and she, even as she died, took care to fall
Becomingly, hiding what should be hidden from men's view.

Then, when the deadly stroke had ended her last breath,
Each Argive there found his own way to do her honour.

Some strewed fresh leaves over her body; some brought
   boughs
And built a pyre; while those who stood with empty hands
Were roundly abused. 'What do you mean,' the others cried,
'By bringing nothing for Polyxena? Have you
No dress, no ornament to offer in her honour?
Hers was the most courageous, noble heart of all.'

So that is how your daughter died. Of all women
You have the noblest children, and the cruellest fate.
CHORUS: What suffering has overwhelmed both Priam's house
   And Troy. The gods impose this; there is no escape.
HECABE: My child! So many pains are here, I cannot tell
   Which one to ponder. If I turn my mind to this,
That other will not let me; and from that a third
Agony again distracts me, grief succeeding grief.
And now, the thought of your cruel end obsesses me;
Yet, though I must mourn for you, you have taken away
The bitterest pain; for you died royally, they say.

How strange, that bad soil, if the gods send rain and sun,
Bears a rich crop, while good soil, starved of what it needs,
Is barren; but *man's* nature is ingrained – the bad
Is never anything but bad, and the good man
Is good: misfortune cannot warp his character,
His goodness will endure.
                  Where lies the difference?
In heredity, or upbringing? Being nobly bred
At least instructs a child in goodness; and this lesson,
If well learnt, shows him by that measure, what evil is.
Oh! These thoughts probe this way and that: what help are
   they?

Talthybius, take this message for me to the Greeks:
To let my daughter lie untouched, and keep them all

Away from her. Soldiers and seamen are a rough
Undisciplined crew, and in their thousands savager
Than fire; and good behaviour only earns abuse.

[*Exit* TALTHYBIUS. HECABE *turns to the old Attendant.*]

Listen, old servant. Take a jar down to the shore,
Fill it with fresh sea-water and bring it. I must go
To wash my daughter's body and compose her limbs;
And to a wedded virgin, an unwedded bride,
Pay the last honours. To do this as she deserves
I have no means or power; but what I can, I will.
And to adorn her – I'll ask my fellow-prisoners
If some of them have jewellery from their own homes
Which they have kept out of the sight of our new masters;
And what they have, they'll all give for Polyxena.

O stately royal palace! O once happy home!
O Priam, famed for boundless treasures; famed as father,
And I as aged mother, of children without peer!
How we have come to nothing, stripped of our old
    pride!
And we – we paltry humans – swell with arrogance,
One for the wealth and luxury of his house, another
Because the citizens all call him a great man!
Such things mean nothing; careful schemes, the eloquence
Of boasters – all nothing! The man who day by day
Lives on, escaping misery – he is happiest.

HECABE goes in.

CHORUS:
    My slavery was ordained,
    The ruin of my life made inevitable,
    On the day when Paris prince of Troy
    Had timber felled in the pine-woods of Mount Ida
    To build a ship for his voyage to Greece,
    To win the bed of Helen, the loveliest woman
    That ever lived in the light of the golden sun.

Now pain and cruel compulsion
Are round us in an unbreakable ring.
By one man's folly a whole nation,
All who drink from the river Simois,
Are destroyed and die together
At the onset of aliens.

The judgement made on Mount Ida,
When the quarrel of three immortal goddesses
Was settled by a herdsman –
That word brought war and slaughter
And the ravaging of my home.

And not only here; but by the clear Eurotas
Some Spartan wife is sitting in her house
Lost in tears and groans;
And a grey-haired mother beats her head
In grief for her dead sons,
And tears her cheek till her nails are stained with blood.

Enter the OLD ATTENDANT, *from the shore; behind her are others,
bearing a draped body.*

ATTENDANT: Women, where's Hecabe – poor, unhappy
  Hecabe?
  No man or woman born has ever suffered so;
  She holds the crown, and no one else can rival her.
CHORUS: What now? Your fateful clamour brings a curse
  with it.
  Do cruel messages never rest? Must you add more?
ATTENDANT: My cruel message is for Hecabe. It's hard
  To avoid unlucky words, with trouble on every side.
CHORUS: See! Hecabe is coming out. Tell her your news.
ATTENDANT: Oh, Hecabe, what sorrow you endure! And now
  The last and worst has happened; you have nothing left –
  Child, husband, city; light and life and all are gone.
HECABE: Your harsh news is not new to me; I know it all.

But why do you bring here my dead Polyxena?
They said the Greeks were busy building her a tomb.
ATTENDANT [*to Chorus*]: She doesn't know; she's thinking of Polyxena,

Poor soul. She has not yet begun to feel this blow.
HECABE: O gods, who is it? Is it Apollo's devotee,
The prophetess? Is it Cassandra you have brought?
ATTENDANT: Cassandra lives; but here, still waiting for your tears,

Is death. Let me uncover his poor body. Look!
There is a face you know, and never thought to see.
HECABE: It is my son. It is Polydorus. He is dead.
I sent him to that Thracian, to keep safe for me.
My wretched life is over. Oh, what shall I do?
    O darling son!
    The dirge I chant for you is inspired;
    For I knew of this already –
    It was told me in a dream
    By the fiend who torments us all.
ATTENDANT: Poor Hecabe! You already knew your son was dead?
HECABE:
    I heard it, but I did not believe it.
    Now I see it, and still I do not believe it.
    Pain follows pain;
    Never one day free from groaning and tears.
CHORUS: O Hecabe, what terrible things happen to us!
HECABE:
    O Polydorus, my poor child,
    What cruel death came to you?
    What pitiful doom struck you down?
    Who can have killed you?
ATTENDANT: I know nothing. I found him lying on the shore.
HECABE: Had the sea cast him up on to the smooth sand?
    Or did he fall by the sword?

ATTENDANT: The waves had carried him up from the sea.

HECABE:

    Oh, now I understand the dream I had;
    The black-winged figure that stood before my eyes
    Was clearly telling me that you, my son,
    No longer lived in the light of day.

CHORUS: Who killed him? Can your skill in dreams interpret
    that?

HECABE:

    It was my own trusted friend,
    The Thracian horseman, to whose house
    Priam had sent him secretly.

CHORUS: Polymestor killed him! Why? To get the gold
    himself?

HECABE: A crime without a name; a sacrilege; an act
    Outstripping speech, or wonder, or endurance. Where
    Is friendship's honour now? O loathed and outcast man!
    Look at this boy's flesh,
    Chopped and carved with your steel blade!
    Had you no pity?

CHORUS: Surely, of all the human race you suffer most,
    Hecabe, by Heaven's will; so great a load you bear.
    Friends, no more words; here comes our master, Agamem-
    non.

Enter AGAMEMNON, *from the camp.*

AGAMEMNON: Why do you not come, Hecabe? Talthybius
    Gave me your message, that no Greek should touch your
      daughter,
    Since you would bury her. So we have left her there un-
      touched;
    And now your long delay is a surprise to me.
    Go now. We have made what arrangements we thought
      good –
    If in this sorry business anything is good.
    – Why, what is this dead body doing near my tent? –

Trojan, to judge by what he's wrapped in; not a Greek.

HECABE: Hecabe, my own most wretched self, what shall I
do?

Kneel before Agamemnon? Or bear all in silence?

AGAMEMNON: Why do you stand there mourning, with your
back to me,

Instead of saying what has happened? Who is this?

HECABE: He may look on me as a slave and enemy,

And push me from him; so I shall add pain to pain.

AGAMEMNON: What's in your mind? I am no soothsayer, to
trace

The path your thoughts are following, unless you tell me.

HECABE: This man should hate me; yet my reckoning may
well

Be wrong. Perhaps he is no enemy after all.

AGAMEMNON: If you prefer to tell me nothing of all this –

Agreed; I am equally prepared to hear nothing.

HECABE: Without his help I cannot ever hope to avenge

My murdered son. Why do I hesitate like this?

I must speak boldly, whether I succeed or fail.

[*She kneels.*]

Agamemnon, I am your suppliant, beseeching you

By knees, and beard, and your victorious right hand –

AGAMEMNON: What is it you desire? Are you requesting me

To grant you freedom? That is readily bestowed.

HECABE: Not freedom, no; but vengeance on a murderer.

To gain that, I'll accept an age of slavery.

AGAMEMNON: What kind of help, then, do you want?

HECABE: Not, Agamemnon,

Such help as you think I would ask. You see this body

That I was weeping over?

AGAMEMNON: Yes; what follows now?

HECABE: This boy I carried in my womb; he was my son.

AGAMEMNON: Poor Hecabe! Then which of all your sons
is this?

HECABE: Not one of those who died before the walls of
    Troy.

AGAMEMNON: Why, had you others?

HECABE: This. Now he is lost to me.

AGAMEMNON: Where was he when the city fell?

HECABE: To save his life
    His father had sent him out of Troy.

AGAMEMNON: Alone, of all
    His brothers?

HECABE: Yes.

AGAMEMNON: Where did he send him?

HECABE: Here to Thrace;
    And here he is discovered, dead.

AGAMEMNON: Was it the king
    You sent him to, Polymestor?

HECABE: Yes, to Polymestor.
    We sent gold with him; that cost him his life.

AGAMEMNON: Why, what
    Happened to him? Who murdered him?

HECABE: Who? Why, who else?
    Our Thracian friend.

AGAMEMNON: A murderer! All to get the gold?

HECABE: Yes, when he learnt that Troy had fallen.

AGAMEMNON: Who brought him here?
    Where was he found?

HECABE: This woman found him on the shore.

AGAMEMNON: Looking for him, or at some other task?

HECABE: She went
    To bring me sea-water, to wash my daughter's body.

AGAMEMNON: It looks as if your friend killed him and cast
    him out.

HECABE: First hacked his flesh, then threw him in the sea to
    drift.

AGAMEMNON: Poor Hecabe! What boundless suffering you
    have borne!

HECABE: My heart is dead now; there is no heart left to suffer.

AGAMEMNON: Was ever any woman so misused by Chance?

HECABE: None, unless Misery be herself a woman. But now,
Listen to my request, for which I kneel to you.
If what I suffer seems to you my just desert,
I accept it. But if not, then help me take revenge
On this most false and perjured friend, who without fear
Of powers below or powers above, has done a deed
Of blackest treachery! Many times he was my guest,
Sat at my table, was among my closest friends,
Was treated with all honour. Then he lays a plot,
And murders. Then, on top of murder, he denies
Even a grave, and throws my son into the sea!

I am a slave, I may be feeble; but the gods
Are strong, and strong is the great Law that governs them.
It is by Law that we believe the gods exist;
By Law we live, by Law distinguish right and wrong.
If Law stands at your bar and is dishonoured there,
If men kill guests, rob temples and are not condemned
And punished, there is no more justice on the earth.
Then let shame guide and honour stir you to my cause.
Look at me: here you see the face of misery;
Stand back and view it like a painter. Pity me.
I was a queen, now I'm your slave; a mother once
With many sons and daughters, now childless and old,
Cityless, friendless, the most wretched of mankind.

– For pity's sake, why do you turn away from me?
My words, my tears, will achieve nothing – I despair!
Why have I not learnt to persuade? What fools we are –
We learn all other skills, take pains, devote ourselves
To study – but Persuasion, queen of human arts,
Which we should search for, and pay fees for, if we hope
Ever to sway men's mind, and get what we desire –

This sovereign knowledge we neglect. How can we hope,
Then, for achievement or success?

                              My sons all gone;
And I dishonoured, carried off a prisoner,
Watching the smoke that curls and billows over Troy!
[*To herself*] I still have one more argument; it may not work,
But yet I'll try it; he is not immune to love.
– Agamemnon, by your side in bed my daughter lies,
Cassandra, whom the Trojans call Apollo's mouth.
Your nights are sweetly spent, Agamemnon, are they not?
Shall not my daughter for her warm embraces earn
Some thanks from you? and shall not she have thanks from
    me?
Listen then: see this dead boy – he is close to you
In blood. His rights are kinsman's rights: then honour them!

Hear my last word now: oh, if I but had a tongue
In every part – in arms and hands and hair and feet,
Moved by such art as Daedalus or a god might wield –
So that together all might clasp your knees and weep,
Battering your heart with varied eloquence! My lord,
Great light of Hellas, hear me! I am an old woman
Of no regard – yet, lend me your avenging hand!
It is a good man's duty to uphold the right,
And always, everywhere, to punish wickedness.
CHORUS: Strange how in human life opposites coincide;
    How love and hate change with the laws men recognize,
    Which can turn bitter foes to friends, old friends to foes.
AGAMEMNON: Your great misfortunes, Hecabe, your mur-
    dered son,
    And your appeal for help, all move me. I would like
    To satisfy both justice and the gods, and make
    This murderous friend of yours pay fitly for his crime,
    If we could find some way to carry out your wish

Without letting the army think I have connived
At killing Polymestor for Cassandra's love.
One point disturbs me specially: the Greeks regard
This Polymestor as an ally, and your son
As an enemy; the fact that he's your son does not
Concern them. So think what you'd better do. You'll find
    me
Eager to help you, but slow to take any step
Likely to invite criticism from the Greeks.

HECABE: A free man? -- There is no such thing! All men are
    slaves;
Some, slaves of money; some, of chance; others are forced,
Either by mass opinion, or the threatening law,
To act against their nature. – Then since you're afraid
And hold the rabble's voices in such high regard,
I will release you from all danger in my project
To punish my son's murderer. Know what I do,
But take no hand in it. And when this Thracian gets
The punishment he will get, if the Achaeans raise
A riot, or gather to his aid, hold them in check.
For the rest, don't worry; I will see to everything.

AGAMEMNON: But how? What will you do? Can *you* handle
    a sword
And kill a Thracian? Or will you poison him? What help,
What ally can you hope for? Have you any friends?

HECABE: The Trojan women in this tent. There's quite a
    crowd.
With them to help me, I'll deal with my murderer.

AGAMEMNON: Those women prisoners? Can they overpower
    a man?

HECABE: Numbers and cunning joined are irresistible.

AGAMEMNON: Numbers, maybe: but women – can't do any-
    thing!

HECABE: No? Did not women kill Aegyptus' fifty sons?
Was it not women who stripped Lemnos clear of males?

However, let us leave this argument. And now
Provide this woman with safe-conduct through the camp.
          [*She turns to the old Attendant.*]
Go with this message to my Thracian friend: 'Hecabe,
Once Queen of Troy, begs you to come, and bring your
     sons.
She has something to tell you which concerns both you
And them, more than herself; so they must hear it too.'
          [*Exit* ATTENDANT.]
Agamemnon, delay the burial of Polyxena,
That I may place brother and sister, my double loss,
Upon one pyre, and lay their ashes in one grave.

AGAMEMNON: It shall be as you ask; though, had the wind
     been fair,
And the fleet sailing, I could not have done this for you.
But since the gods send us rough weather, we're com-
     pelled
To wait. I hope all this will turn out for the best.
It is important both for individuals
And for the State in general, that the wrongdoer
Should suffer, and the honest man reap his reward.

     HECABE *goes in.* AGAMEMNON *returns to the camp.*

CHORUS:
     Troy, my fathers' home! No longer
     Will you be named among cities never sacked.
     A thundercloud of Greeks hides you from sight,
     And their spears have destroyed you.
     You are shorn of your crown of towers,
     Your ravaged face marked with the grime of smoke.
     Poor Troy, I shall never walk in you again.

     Midnight was my moment of death,
     The hour when, after supper,
     Sweet sleep is shed upon all eyes;
     The songs were over; my husband

Had brought to an end the rejoicing and the sacrifice,
And was lying on his bed;
His spear hung on the nail;
Swarms of foreign sailors were no more to be seen
Trampling the plain of Troy.

I was arranging my hair,
Fastening it under my cap,
Gazing in the endless gleam of my golden mirror,
Sitting ready to fall into my bed;
When a roar rose along the streets,
And through the city of Troy we heard this war-cry:
'Now is the time, men of Hellas!
Sack the fortress of Troy, and you'll all go home!'

I left my bed – my dear bed –
And wearing only a gown, like a Spartan girl,
I sat, a trembling suppliant, at the altar of Artemis;
But the altar did not save me.
I saw my husband killed.
Then I was brought here by sea;
And when the ship was under way, heading for Hellas,
Parting me from my native soil,
I looked back through my tears at Troy,
Fainting with anguish;

And I called down a curse on Helen,
Sister of the Heavenly Twins,
And on the herdsman of Ida, Paris the plague of Troy,
Because it was their marriage –
No marriage, but the raging of a fiend of Fate –
That uprooted me from my home
And sent me from Troy to slavery.
I pray that Helen may never reach her father's house,
But be drowned in the salt sea.

Enter, from the tent, HECABE; *from the direction of the camp,*
   POLYMESTOR *with his two young sons and several guards.*

POLYMESTOR: O Priam, dearest friend! Hecabe, no less dear!
   The fate that you and Troy have suffered, and the death
   Of your dear daughter, bring the tears into my eyes.
   Nothing is lasting; fair fame and prosperity
   Alike may be reversed. The gods dispose our fortunes
   This way and that in sheer confusion, so that we
   May reverence them through fear of the unknown. And yet,
   What is the use of lamentation? It helps no one
   To overcome his troubles. When you first arrived
   I was away up-country, as it happened; so if
   You felt hurt that I did not come to visit you,
   Forgive me. As soon as I returned, I was on the point
   Of coming, when your servant met me at the door
   And gave your message, which I obeyed; and here I am.

HECABE: I am so crushed, Polymestor, with calamity,
   That I scarcely know how to look you in the face.
   You knew me in my palace; to confront you now,
   A prisoner, fills me with confusion. If my eyes
   Do not meet yours directly, that is because deep feeling
   Forbids it; do not take it as ill-will to you,
   Polymestor. Custom too is partly my excuse,
   Which requires women's eyes not to be raised to men.

POLYMESTOR: I fully understand. But tell me, why did you
   Send for me to come here? What can I do for you?

HECABE: I have something to say to you and to your sons
   In private. Tell your bodyguard to wait outside.

POLYMESTOR [*to guards*]: Go outside. It's quite safe, there's
   no one else about.
                    [*They go.*]
   [*To Hecabe*] You are my friend, and the Greek army are my
   friends.
   Now tell me, what can one whose life is prosperous
   Do for a friend in trouble? I am at your command.

HECABE: First tell me of Polydorus, whom his father and I
   Entrusted to your care. Is he alive? The rest
   I'll ask you later.

POLYMESTOR: Of course! Have no fears about him.

HECABE: What welcome words! You speak like the true friend
   you are.

POLYMESTOR: What's your next question?

HECABE: Does my son remember me?

POLYMESTOR: Yes; his wish was to come here to you
   secretly.

HECABE: And is the gold safe, which he brought with him
   from Troy?

POLYMESTOR: Safe in my palace, closely guarded.

HECABE: Keep it safe;
   And don't be covetous.

POLYMESTOR: I will not. I hope rather
   To have the quiet enjoyment of what is my own.

HECABE: Now this is what I want to tell you and your sons –

POLYMESTOR: What is it? Tell me.

HECABE: To a friend so dear as you
   I would entrust –

POLYMESTOR: Yes? What?

HECABE: There is a store of gold,
   Heirlooms of Priam's family, buried long ago.

POLYMESTOR: You're asking me to tell your son about this
   gold?

HECABE: Yes, you must tell him. You're a man who fears the
   gods.

POLYMESTOR: Why did you want my sons to hear about it
   too?

HECABE: Suppose you died: it would be better they should
   know.

POLYMESTOR: You are right, it's wiser.

HECABE: Do you know the place in Troy
   Where once Athene's temple stood?

POLYMESTOR: The gold is there?
Is there some mark to trace it by?
HECABE: Yes, a black rock
Jutting above ground level.
POLYMESTOR: Are there other things
You want to tell me about this treasure?
HECABE: Yes; I brought
Certain things with me when I came away. I want
You to take charge of them.
POLYMESTOR: Where are they hidden? Do you
Carry them on you? or keep them somewhere?
HECABE: In that tent;
They're hidden under a pile of armour.
POLYMESTOR: What? In there?
So close to the Achaean ships?
HECABE: None of their men
Enter our living quarters. We are private here.
POLYMESTOR: I see; so it's quite safe?
HECABE: We women prisoners
Are not disturbed. Come in. The Greeks are in a hurry
To spread their sails for home. So when your business here
Is duly done, you and your children may together
Set out for that place where you gave my son a home.

POLYMESTOR *and his two sons enter the tent,* followed by
HECABE.

CHORUS:
The moment for paying your debt has not yet come,
But it will come.
As a man falls sideways into deep water
And finds no foothold,
So you will fall from the desire of your heart,
And forfeit your life.
There is a debt to Justice, and a debt to the gods;
Where these two coincide
The payment is final and complete.

You made this journey in hope, but hope shall deceive you,
Leading your wretched life to its end in death.
The weak shall be too strong for you,
The unwarlike shall overcome you.

POLYMESTOR [*within*]: Help, help! They are blinding me!

CHORUS: You heard, friends? That was the Thracian king.

POLYMESTOR [*within*]: Help! Save my children! They are murdering them!

CHORUS: Friends, terrible things have been done.

POLYMESTOR [*within*]: You may run away, but you shan't escape.
  I'll smash everything, I'll tear the place down.

CHORUS: Listen to him! He's terribly strong and violent.
  Ought we to rush in, do you think, and try to help
  Hecabe and the others? They are in great danger.

Enter HECABE.

HECABE: Rage as you will, tear down the walls, batter the doors.
  You'll never put the sight back in your darkened eyes,
  Nor see your sons again alive, whom I have killed.

CHORUS: What? Did you truly overpower him and destroy him,
  Mistress? And did you do in fact what you have said?

HECABE: You will soon see him for yourselves. He will come out,
  A blind man blindly groping his way; and you shall see
  The bodies of his two sons, whom I killed, with the help
  Of those brave women. I have my revenge on him.
  Look, here he comes. I'll stand aside out of his way;
  He's in a boiling Thracian rage, and dangerous.

Enter POLYMESTOR, *blinded*.

POLYMESTOR:
  Help! Where can I go?
  Where can I stand for safety?
  Must I crawl on my hands like a four-footed beast,

Tracking them out? Where shall I turn –
This way, that way? I must catch them,
Murderous Trojan hags, who have destroyed me!
Curse them, curse them, brazen Phrygian beasts!
Where are they hiding from me? Where are they
    skulking?
O Sun! I am blind!
Can't you, can't you heal me,
Put back the light into my bleeding eyes?

Ah! Hush! I heard a stealthy step –
That's one of them! If I catch her
I'll tear her flesh and break her bones,
I'll make my meal on these savage beasts;
I'll do to them what they've done to me,
I'll have my revenge.

Where can I go? Must I leave my children
To be torn in pieces by fiends of death?
Leave them as food for dogs,
Their bleeding flesh cast on the mountain-side?
Where can I furl sail like a sea-going ship?
Where can I stop and rest?
Let me find the place where my dead children lie,
And fly there to protect them!

CHORUS: Wretched man, your agony is hard to bear;
    But when crime is atrocious punishment will be heavy.

POLYMESTOR:

Thracians! Hear me, Thracians!
Come with your spears, your armour, your horses!
Thracian warriors, hearts of Ares!
Help, Achaeans! Help, sons of Atreus!
Help, I call for help!
Come, in the name of the gods!
Do you hear me? Is no one coming? Where are you?

These women have murdered me!
Look what they've done to me,
These women, your prisoners!

Where can I turn, where can I go?
Oh, if I could fly to the high palace of heaven,
Where fiery Sirius and Orion stream light from their
    eyes –
Or must I plunge in despair
Down to the dark crossing and the river of death?

CHORUS: When a man's sufferings are more than he can bear,
It is pardonable to end at once a wretched life.

Enter AGAMEMNON, *attended.*

AGAMEMNON: I heard a fearful shouting. All about the
    camp
Echo, child of the mountain cliff, was clamouring,
Spreading disturbance. Had we not been sure that Troy
Was captured by Greek arms, and all her walls laid flat,
A noise like this would have produced a panic.

POLYMESTOR: Ah!
My dearest friend, Agamemnon! Yes, I know your voice.
Do you see what they have done to me?

AGAMEMNON: Why, Polymestor!
What brought you to this state? Your eyes! Who blinded
    you?
Who killed these children? Whoever perpetrated this
Must have felt fearful anger against you and them.

POLYMESTOR: Hecabe did it – she and your women
    prisoners;
She murdered me – no, worse than murder; much, much
    worse.

AGAMEMNON: What, Hecabe? Is this the truth? Impossible!
You yourself, Hecabe, dared to carry out this act?

POLYMESTOR: What's that? Is Hecabe there near me?
    Where is she?

97

Quick, show me, tell me, let me get my hands on her,
I'll rip her into rags.

AGAMEMNON: Here, now, stay where you are.

POLYMESTOR: For God's sake let me get at her, or I'll go
mad.

AGAMEMNON: Control yourself. Forget you're a bar-
barian,
And state your case. I'll hear both you and her in turn,
And justly judge the causes that have led to this.

POLYMESTOR: I'll tell you. Hecabe had a son called Poly-
dorus,
Her youngest. Priam sent him away from Troy to me,
To bring up in my house, since he was much afraid
Troy would be captured. Well, I killed him. Why I did,
How rightly and prudently I acted, I'll explain.
I feared that this boy – your enemy – if left alive,
Might gather Troy's survivors and re-found the city;
And then the Achaeans, learning that one of Priam's sons
Was still alive, would bring an army here again,
And tramp all over Thrace, stealing and plundering,
And we, Troy's neighbours, would then suffer yet again
What we've put up with all these years. Well, Hecabe
Found out her son was dead, and lured me here with tales
Of gold treasured by Priam's family, still buried
Under Troy's ruins. So that no one else might know,
She brought me alone into the tent with my two sons.
I sat there at my ease in the middle of the couch,
And all those Trojan women sat, some on my left,
Some on my right, as if I was a friend, admiring
The Thracian texture of my cloak, holding it up
To catch the light. Others were looking at my spears;
And so I was disarmed of both. Those who were mothers
Lifted my children in their arms, admiring them,
And passed them on from one to another, to make sure
They were far away from me.

98

                              Then suddenly, in the midst
Of all this gentle talk – can you imagine it? –
They whipped out daggers from their clothes and stabbed
   my sons.
Some of them in a mass fell on my arms and legs.
I tried to go to help my sons; lifted my head –
They held me down by the hair. I tried to move my hands;
I could do nothing against twenty women. At last –
And worse than all before – they did a ghastly thing:
They took their brooches, and they stabbed and tore my eyes –
Oh, my poor eyes! And then they fled away from me.
I leapt up like a wild beast and went after them –
Bloodthirsty bitches – like a hunter, searching round
Along the walls, shaking and battering. And this
Is what I've suffered in your cause, for killing one
Who was your enemy, Agamemnon. To be brief,
I'll say just this: all the abuse that men have heaped
On women in time past, all they are saying now
Or ever will say, I can sum it in one phrase:
No monster like a woman breeds in land or sea;
And those who have most to do with women know it best.
CHORUS: Because you suffer, why should you so arrogantly
   Include all women in one general reproach?
HECABE: It is deplorable, Agamemnon, that men's words
   Should ever seem to speak more loudly than their deeds.
   Good deeds alone should make the doer eloquent,
   And bad deeds dress themselves in rotten arguments,
   Not gloze their foulness with fair colours. There are men
   Who make this practice a fine art. Their cleverness,
   So-called, cannot last long; they all, without exception,
   Come to a bad end. Thus much I address to you,
   Agamemnon; now I turn to him, and point by point
   I answer him.

                    – You say, it was to save the Greeks
   A double labour, serving Agamemnon's cause,

That you murdered my son. In the first place, how could
Your savage nation ever be a friend to Hellas?
Next, whence arose this fervent zeal to help the Greeks?
Are you related to them? Did you hope to be –
Some marriage-scheme, perhaps? What *was* the reason,
   then?
A second expedition might have spoilt your crops,
You say? Who do you imagine you'll convince of that?
Why not agree to tell the truth? It was the gold,
The gold and your own greed, that cost my son his life.
Come, explain this: how was it, that when Troy was strong,
Defended round with ramparts, Priam still alive,
And Hector's sword triumphant, when my son was living
As guest in your house – why did you not kill him then,
Or hand him to the Greeks alive, if you were anxious
To curry favour with Agamemnon? But when we
Had fallen on dark days, when the smoke of Troy pro-
   claimed
Our enemies' triumph, then you killed the guest who came
To sit at your hearth.

                    That's not all; here's more to prove
Your wickedness. This gold, which you admit belonged
To my son, not to you – you ought to have taken it,
If you were the Achaeans' friend, and given it to them.
They were in great need, being so long away from home.
But no – even now you cannot bear to let it go;
You've still got it at home. And yet – suppose you had given
My son the care and love you should have given him,
Everyone would have praised you as a loyal friend
Who showed his worth – not in prosperity, when friends
Are cheap, but in defeat and ruin. And my son,
If you had fallen on poverty, and he was rich,
Would have stood by you, been a storehouse for your need.
But now you have not Polydorus for a friend;

The gold is useless to you; you have lost your sons;
And you are blind.

             – Agamemnon, if you help this man,
You help an impious, perjured, and polluted traitor,
And by upholding evil soil your own fair name.
Yet – you're my master; and I'll moderate my words.

CHORUS: A good cause provides matter for an honest speech.

AGAMEMNON: I find it irksome to judge other men's mis-
    deeds;
But yet I must. I undertook to hear this cause,
And therefore cannot honourably abandon it.
I judge, then, Polymestor, thus: that it was not
For my sake or the Achaeans' that you killed your guest;
But so that you might keep this gold in your own house.
Your present plight prompted your plausible defence.
Perhaps in Thrace to kill a guest is a light matter;
In Hellas we regard it as a wicked crime.
If I pronounced you innocent, I should be myself
Guilty. Your crime was foul; you must endure your fate.

POLYMESTOR: My fate, indeed! Trampled on, outraged by
    a woman!
A king – submitting to the vengeance of a slave!

HECABE: You suffer justly what your wickedness deserved.

POLYMESTOR: Oh, my poor murdered children! Oh, my
    ruined eyes!

HECABE: You suffer – what then? Do I not suffer for my
    son?

POLYMESTOR: Blood-guilty wretch! You take a joy in
    mocking me.

HECABE: I have punished you; therefore my joy is justified.

POLYMESTOR: It will not last much longer; the sea waits
    for you.

HECABE: To carry me to Hellas?

POLYMESTOR: No; to cover you,
When you fall headlong from the mast.

HECABE: And who will force
Me to perform so wild a leap?

POLYMESTOR: Why, you yourself
Will climb up to the masthead.

HECABE: How? Shall I have wings?

POLYMESTOR: You will become a dog with glaring tawny
eyes.

HECABE: How do you know that I shall change my shape?

POLYMESTOR: In Thrace
We have a prophet, Dionysus. He told me.

HECABE: Did he not warn you of what would happen to you
today?

POLYMESTOR: No, or your trickery would not have trapped
me so.

HECABE: And shall I die, or live my life out?

POLYMESTOR: You shall die.
Your tomb shall bear your name.

HECABE: A name to signify
My transformation?

POLYMESTOR: Cynossema, the Dog's Grave;
A sign for sailors.

HECABE: I care nothing. I am avenged.

POLYMESTOR: There's more to tell. Cassandra shall be
murdered too.

HECABE: No! Never! May the gods fulfil such words for *you*!

POLYMESTOR: Agamemnon's wife, who waits implacably at
home,
Shall kill her.

HECABE: Gods prevent such madness!

POLYMESTOR: She shall raise
Her axe on high, and murder Agamemnon too.

AGAMEMNON: Here – are you mad? or asking for more
punishment?

POLYMESTOR: Kill me. A bloody cleansing waits for you in
Argos.

AGAMEMNON: Men, hold this fellow, take him away.

POLYMESTOR: You don't enjoy
Learning the future?

AGAMEMNON: Gag him!

POLYMESTOR: Gag me. I have spoken.

AGAMEMNON: Take him at once and throw him on some
desert island.

Intolerable insolence!

> [*Exeunt Guards with* POLYMESTOR.]
> Poor Hecabe!

Go now and bury your two children. You other women,
Go each of you to your new master's tent. I see
That a fair wind is springing up to take us home.
Heaven grant us now deliverance from all our troubles,
A prosperous voyage, and peace and happiness at home!

CHORUS:

Friends, we must go to the harbour and the Achaean
tents;
Now we are to know the rigours of slavery.
Fate compels, and none can resist.

> *Exeunt omnes.*

ELECTRA

*

Characters:

A PEASANT *of Mycenae*
ELECTRA, *daughter of Agamemnon*
ORESTES, *son of Agamemnon*
PYLADES, *friend of Orestes*
CHORUS *of country women of Mycenae*
AN OLD MAN, *once a servant of Agamemnon*
A MESSENGER
CLYTEMNESTRA, *widow of Agamemnon*
THE DIOSCORI, *Castor and Polydeuces, sons of Zeus*

*

*The scene is outside the Peasant's cottage. It is night, a little before
sunrise.*

Enter the PEASANT, *from the cottage.*

PEASANT: Argos the ancient! River Inachus! It was here
That once King Agamemnon led his army forth
And with his thousand ships of war set sail for Troy;
And having killed Priam the king of Troy, and sacked
The noble city Dardanus founded, he returned
Home here to Argos, and on our temple walls hung high
His countless trophies taken from a barbarous race.
Abroad, he had good fortune; here in his own home
He died, by his wife Clytemnestra's treachery
And by Aegisthus' murderous hand, Thyestes' son.

So Agamemnon, parted from the ancient throne
Of Tantalus, is dead; Aegisthus is king now;
And Clytemnestra, Agamemnon's wife, is now
Aegisthus' wife. As for the children who were left

At home when the king went to Troy – the son, Orestes,
Aegisthus was resolved to kill; but an old slave
Who had once looked after the boy's father, took him off
To Phocis, and gave him to Strophius to bring up.
Electra stayed at home; when she was marriageable,
And nobles from all Hellas came to beg her hand,
Aegisthus, fearing, if her husband were a prince,
Her son would take revenge for Agamemnon's death,
Kept her at home, and would let no one marry her.

But this plan too seemed dangerous; she might bear a son
In secret to some man of noble blood. Therefore
Aegisthus planned to kill her. Clytemnestra then,
Cruel as she is, stopped him, and saved Electra's life.
She could claim reason for her husband's murder; but
She feared the hatred her child's death would bring on
    her.
Aegisthus then thought out another plan: he promised
To anyone who killed Orestes – now in exile –
A reward of gold; and gave Electra to be wife
To me. Well, I belong to a good family;
I've nothing to be ashamed of there – we're Mycenaeans,
And always have been; but we're poor; and when you're
    poor
Good breeding counts for nothing. So Aegisthus thought,
'Marry her to a nobody – I've nothing to fear.'
A noble husband would go stirring up old blood
Which now lies quiet; Aegisthus then would have to pay
That debt he justly owes for Agamemnon's death.

Well, I'm her husband; but I swear by Aphrodite,
I've not come near her bed; she is a virgin still.
Her father was a king; I'm not her quality;
Therefore I'd be ashamed to take advantage of her.
I'm sorry for Orestes – he's my brother-in-law

  In name! If only one day he'd come home again
  To Argos, and see his sister married, and all well!

  If any man thinks me a fool, for harbouring
  A young girl in my house and never touching her,
  He measures what's right by the wretched standard of
  His own mind; he's a fool himself, I say, and worse.
          Exit PEASANT. *Enter* ELECTRA *from the cottage.*
ELECTRA: O black night, you who nurse the golden stars! In
      you
  I go, bearing this jar poised on my head, to fetch
  Water from springs of rivers; not that any need
  Pushes me to this point, but so that I may show
  The gods the insolence of Aegisthus, and pour out
  My griefs under huge heaven to my father's spirit.
  My mother, Tyndareos' daughter, lost in wickedness,
  To show Aegisthus favour, drives me out of doors.
  And since she has borne Aegisthus other sons, she treats
  Me and Orestes both as bastards of her house.
          The PEASANT *returns.*
PEASANT: Electra, why do you work so hard, all for my sake?
  You were brought up a princess; you're not made for toil.
  I've said this to you often – yet you will not rest.
ELECTRA: To me your kindness is the kindness of the gods;
  You take no advantage of my helpless misery.
  In this life it's a great thing to have found a friend
  To ease one's load of bitterness, as you do mine.
  I know you don't expect it; but it's right that I
  Should do my share, and work with all the strength I have
  To make life easier for you. You have enough
  Work on the farm; to keep things pleasant in the house
  Is my task. When a man comes home from the day's work
  He likes to find the house tidy and comfortable.
PEASANT: Go, then, if you wish; the well is not so far away.
  As soon as it grows light I'll take the oxen out

And do some harrowing. Pious words and idle hands
Bring in no breakfast.

Exeunt ELECTRA *and* PEASANT *severally*.
Enter ORESTES *and* PYLADES.

ORESTES: Pylades, you're the man I trust above all others.
I've shared your home; you're a true friend – the only
  one
Who has honoured me in spite of the condition to which
Aegisthus has reduced me, murdering my father –
He, and my fiendish-hearted mother. Now I have come,
Sent by Apollo's oracle, to Argive soil,
To shed the blood of those who shed my father's blood.
No one knows I am here. Tonight I have visited
My father's grave; I offered tears, and a shorn lock,
And killed a lamb, and let its blood fall on the earth –
All this unknown to those who tyrannize this land.

And now, instead of entering the city walls,
I have come here, near the border, with two ends in view:
First, to escape into some other country, if
A frontier guard should recognize me; secondly,
I am searching for my sister, who, so I am told,
Is married, and lives near. I must confer with her,
And get her help in executing our revenge.
I'll learn from her how matters stand inside the palace.

Look! The bright glance of dawn is rising. Let us leave
This place, and find some ploughman, or some slave-woman,
Whom we can ask whether my sister lives near by.

But wait – I see a slave-girl coming, carrying
A water-jar on her shorn head. Let us keep hidden.
We may get information from her, if she drops
Some word about those matters which have brought us here.

They withdraw to one side. Enter ELECTRA *carrying a jar of water.*

ELECTRA:

Quicken your step; the hour grows late.
Walk weeping as you go,
Weeping, weeping.
Agamemnon was my father;
My mother was Clytemnestra,
The detested daughter of Tyndareos.
I am known to the people of Argos
As 'poor Electra'.
Oh! My misery is unbearable,
My life hateful.
And you, father – there you lie in the world of the dead,
Killed by your wife and her lover:
Agamemnon killed by Aegisthus!

Wake once more the same lament,
Revel in luxury of tears!

The hour is late; quicken your step,
Wailing loudly as you go,
Wailing, weeping as you go.
Brother, what fate is yours?
What city, what house holds you in bondage
Since you left your sister sad in her room at home,
To a future of bitterness and pain?

Come, my brother, save me from misery and weariness!
Zeus, O Zeus, hear me! Let Orestes,
Wherever he be, land on the shore of Argos
And punish the murderers of our father!
            [*A slave appears from the cottage.*]
Take this jar from my head and set it down,
That I may weep for my father
And utter my night-long groanings loud in the morning
    air,

A cry of despair, a song of death.
Father, I call to you in the deep earth;
Hear the lamentation which fills all my days,
As nail tears cheek, and hand beats down
On head shorn in mourning for your death.

Weep, wail, beat the head!
As a swan, singing beside the broad river-reach,
Calls lovingly for her father
Lured to his death in a strangling snare,
So I, father, weep for your dreadful end.

How pitifully you lay in death,
After your last ritual cleansing!
Oh, father, father!
Cruel the axe's edge that cut your flesh,
Cruel the cunning that awaited you
When you finished your journey from Troy,
And your wife welcomed you home
Not with crown or garland
But with a two-edged sword,
To suffer the insults of Aegisthus;
And so won her treacherous lover.

Enter the CHORUS.

CHORUS: Electra, daughter of Agamemnon,
We have come to visit you in your country home.
A man from Mycenae, bred on mountain milk,
Has come to tell us that the people of Argos
Announce a festival for the day after tomorrow;
And all the unmarried girls are getting ready
To walk in procession to Hera's temple.

ELECTRA: Not fine dresses nor necklaces of gold,
Dear friends, make my sad heart beat faster.
I will not set the girls of Argos dancing,
Nor will I twirl and stamp among them.

My nights are drawn out with tears,
My hopeless days are occupied with tears.
Look at me – my hair uncared-for,
My dress in tatters!
Would not his daughter's appearance
Bring shame to King Agamemnon,
And make Troy blush to remember her conqueror?

CHORUS: Hera is great. Do come!
Borrow from me a lovely gown, closely woven,
And a gold necklace – I should be so pleased –
To go with it. Do you expect
Ever to overcome your enemies
If you spend your time in weeping
Instead of honouring the gods?
Your day of happiness, my child, will come
Not from sighs and groans
But from pious prayers to the gods.

ELECTRA: Electra the wretched prays;
Year after year her father's blood cries from the ground;
But no god hears.
Mourn for the king who died,
Mourn for the prince who lives
Exile and outcast in a foreign country,
Serving another man's house for the sake of his roof –
Son of so famous a father!
While I, banished from my ancestral palace,
Live in a labourer's cottage,
Eating out my heart among these bleak crags;
And my mother lies with a new husband
In a bed stained with murder.

CHORUS: Your mother's sister Helen by her guilt has brought
Grief without measure on Hellas and your family.

ORESTES and PYLADES *approach, accompanied by two Attendants.*

ELECTRA: Look, friends! I see two men there! They were
crouching low

And hiding; now they're coming out, towards the house.
They're after no good; quick now, let's get out of their way.
You go by the path, I'll hide indoors.

ORESTES: Don't run away!
What are you afraid of? I won't do you any harm.

ELECTRA: Phoebus Apollo! Don't let them murder me, I
pray!

ORESTES: God grant I kill my enemies. You are no enemy.

ELECTRA: Go away, don't touch me! What right have you to
take my hand?

ORESTES: There's no one living whose hand I have more right
to take.

ELECTRA: Indeed? Then why lurk round my house with your
sword drawn?

ORESTES: Wait, now, and listen. You will soon agree with
me.

ELECTRA: I'm waiting. You're the stronger; I am in your
hands.

ORESTES: I bring news of your brother.

ELECTRA: Oh! You are a friend!
Is he alive – or dead?

ORESTES: Alive. So much is good.

ELECTRA: May happiness reward you for so dear a message.

ORESTES: May happiness indeed come to both you and me.

ELECTRA: Poor, exiled brother! In what land does he live
now?

ORESTES: He goes from city to city, citizen of none.

ELECTRA: Is he in want of daily food?

ORESTES: He is not in want;
But he is a refugee, and powerless.

ELECTRA: What message
From him?

ORESTES: To learn if you are alive; and then, what sort
Of life you have.

ELECTRA: My face is withered, as you see.

ORESTES: Wasted with grief and suffering, as I weep to see.

ELECTRA: I've cut my hair off. Tell him of my Scythian scalp.

ORESTES: – To mark your grief for him, and for your father's
death.

ELECTRA: They are dearer to me than anything in my whole
life.

ORESTES: Do you not think your brother loves you?

ELECTRA: He is not here;
He loves me from a distance.

ORESTES: Tell me, Electra,
What makes you live so far from Argos?

ELECTRA: I came here
When I was married. My marriage is a living death.

ORESTES: I grieve for Orestes. Is your husband a Mycenaean?

ELECTRA: Yes – one my father never hoped to give me to.

ORESTES: Who is he? Tell me, so that I can tell your brother.

ELECTRA: I live in this outlandish place. This is his house.

ORESTES: What, this? A ditcher, or a cowherd, might live
here!

ELECTRA: He's poor, but generous-hearted; and he shows me
reverence.

ORESTES [indignant and resentful]: What sort of reverence does
this husband have for you?

ELECTRA: He knows his place. He has never yet come near
my bed.

ORESTES: Why? For religious reasons? Or perhaps he thinks
You are not worthy of him.

ELECTRA: No; he thinks himself
Unworthy, and does not wish to affront my ancestors.

ORESTES: He's pleased enough, no doubt, to have made such a
marriage?

ELECTRA: He holds, the man who gave me to him had no such
right.

ORESTES: I see; he fears Orestes may yet punish him.

ELECTRA: That too; but he's a man by nature virtuous.

ORESTES: He seems a truly generous man. We should reward
    him.

ELECTRA: We should indeed – if the exile ever returns home.

ORESTES: Your mother – was she content to see you married
    here?

ELECTRA: Friend, women's love is for their lovers, not their
    children.

ORESTES: What made Aegisthus put this outrage on you?

ELECTRA: He hoped
    That, married to a clod, I should bear feeble sons.

ORESTES: – Who would not burn to avenge you?

ELECTRA: Yes, that was his thought.
    I trust he'll pay me for it one day.

ORESTES: Does he know
    You are still a virgin?

ELECTRA: No, we keep him out of that.

ORESTES: These women can hear all we're saying – are they
    friends?

ELECTRA: Yes, to us both; they'll keep our counsel faithfully.

ORESTES: Suppose Orestes comes: how will he deal with
    this?

ELECTRA: You ask that? You insult him. Is the time not ripe?

ORESTES: But, once he came, how could he carry out this
    killing?

ELECTRA: Let him be resolute, as his father's murderers
    were.

ORESTES: Would you be resolute to help him kill your
    mother?

ELECTRA: I would – with the same axe by which my father
    died.

ORESTES: I'll tell him, then, that you are steadfast?

ELECTRA: When I have shed
    Her blood to requite his, then I can die content.

ORESTES [after a pause, realizing that she is twice as resolute as he]:
    I wish Orestes could be by, to hear you speak.

114

ELECTRA: Friend, if I saw him I should not recognize him.

ORESTES: No, naturally; you were both young when you
    were parted.

ELECTRA: Of all my friends there's only one who would know
    him now.

ORESTES: You mean the man who stole him away and saved
    his life?

ELECTRA: Yes, an old man who was my father's tutor once.

ORESTES: Now tell me: was your father given a proper grave?

ELECTRA: His body lies now where it fell, thrown out of
    doors.

ORESTES: No! How unspeakable! – Forgive me; but one feels
    The wound of such a wrong, though not involved oneself.
    For sympathy comes with perception: a brutal man
    Has none; while the perceptive pay a certain price
    For their too keen perception, in their own distress.

    Now tell me of your father's fate, and of your own –
    Unpleasant things to speak of, yet they must be told
    If I'm to take your brother back a full account.

CHORUS: I want to hear this too. Living so far from Argos,
    I don't know all that happened there; now I can learn.

ELECTRA: I'll tell you, since I must – I must, since you're a
    friend –
    About my father's wrongs and mine. Here are the words
    You've asked for: tell Orestes my disgrace and his;
    First, how I'm dressed; how I am stabled here; the filth
    That weighs me down, the squalid shack that has replaced
    My royal palace; how I must sit at the loom and weave
    Cloth for my own dress, or go naked; never a feast
    On holy days, never a dance; I cannot mix
    With wives, myself a virgin; as for Castor, who,
    Before he joined the gods, was courting me, his cousin,
    How can I think of him? Meanwhile my mother sits
    Lapped in the spoils of Troy, and Trojan waiting-maids

My father captured and brought home, stand by her throne,
Their Phrygian gowns buckled with golden clasps. And still
The dark stain of my father's blood lies festering there;
While he who killed him gets into my father's own
Chariot, and rides forth and back, and swaggeringly
Grasps in his bloody hand the very sceptre which
My father carried when he led Hellas to war.
On Agamemnon's grave no wine was ever yet
Poured out, no wreath of myrtle laid; dishonoured, bare
Of pious adornment, there it lies. My mother's husband,
Royal Aegisthus, when he's drunk, so people say,
Jumps on the grave, or flings stones at my father's name
Inscribed there, and shouts words intended for us all,
Such as, 'Where is your son Orestes? Should he not
Be here, to ensure proper protection for your tomb?'
The insult goes unanswered; Orestes is not here.

So, friend, I beg you, tell him everything I've said.
The message comes from many; I speak one for all –
My hands, my tongue, my anguished heart, my close-cropped head,
And, most of all, *his* father. Agamemnon brought
Death to the Phrygian nation: Orestes is still young,
And had a greater father – can't he kill one man?
CHORUS: Electra, look! I see your husband coming back;
  He has left his work, and is hurrying towards the house.
                    Enter the PEASANT.
PEASANT: Well! Who are these two strangers I see by the door?
  Now what should bring them to a country place like this?
  Is it me the gentlemen were wanting? – Now look, wife:
  It's not right to stand talking out here with young men.
ELECTRA: Dear husband, don't think any wrong of me. I'll tell you

116

Just what has happened: these two men have brought me
    word
Of Orestes. – Friends, forgive the way he spoke to you.

PEASANT: Well, what news have they brought? Is Orestes still
    alive?

ELECTRA: They say so, and I believe them.

PEASANT: Does he bear in mind
    Your father's wrongs, and yours?

ELECTRA: We can do no more than hope;
    A stateless man has few resources.

PEASANT: What do they say
    Of him?

ELECTRA: He sent them to spy out my desolate life.

PEASANT: Then some of it they've seen, the rest no doubt
    you've told them.

ELECTRA: They know; I've told them everything.

PEASANT: Then why's the door
    Still shut? You ought to have asked them in. – Sirs, come
    inside.
    For your good news, such entertainment as we have
    Is yours, and welcome. – Men, bring all their traps indoors.
    – Now don't say no; you're friends, and you've come from
    a friend.
    I've been a poor man all my life, but I'm not mean.

ORESTES: By the gods! Is this the man whose loyalty has made
    Your marriage no marriage, to save Orestes' honour?

ELECTRA: This is the man who is known as 'poor Electra's
    husband'.

ORESTES: Well!
    There's no clear sign to tell the quality of a man;
    Nature and place turn vice and virtue upside down.
    I've seen a noble father breed a worthless son,
    And good sons come of evil parents; a starved soul
    Housed in a rich man's palace, a great heart dressed in
    rags.

By what sign, then, shall one tell good from bad? By wealth?
Wealth's a false standard. By possessing nothing, then?
No; poverty is a disease; and want itself
Trains men in crime. Or must I look to see how men
Behave in battle? When you're watching your enemy's spear
You don't know who's brave, who's a coward. The best way
Is to judge each man as you find him; there's no rule.

This man is not a leading Argive citizen;
He's not a well-known member of a famous house;
He's one of the many; yet he's a true nobleman.
Then, all you blunderers, full of empty theories,
Why not give up your folly, and judge men's qualities
By the company they keep and by the way they act?

However, since a kind reception's due to both –
To me in person, and in his absence to Orestes
Whose messenger I am – come on, let us accept
This house's hospitality. – Men, go inside.
Give me a host who's poor but friendly, rather than
A rich one. Yet, though I accept his invitation –
Oh! how I wish your brother now, restored and royal,
Were welcoming me into a rejoicing house!
He may yet come. Human prognostications I've
No use for; but Apollo's prophecies are sure.

Exeunt ORESTES *and* PYLADES *with Attendants into the cottage.*

CHORUS: Now more than ever, Electra, my heart warms
     with joy.

   Luck stirs at last, and may soon reach a happy end.

ELECTRA [*to her husband*]: You fool, you know how bare your
     house is. These two guests

   Are far above your level. Why must you ask them in?

PEASANT: Why not? If they're as noble as they look, they'll
     be

   Equally at home in a cottage or anywhere else.

118

ELECTRA: Remember, you're 'the poor'. Still, since you've
    done it now,
    Go quickly and find my father's old servant, who, since
    They turned him out of Argos, tends a flock of sheep
    Close to the Spartan frontier, by the Tanaos;
    Tell him we have guests, and he must come and bring some-
    thing
    That I can cook and give them. He'll be pleased enough
    To know my brother, the child whom he once saved, still
    lives;
    He'll bless the gods. Well, we'd get nothing from my
    mother
    Out of my father's house. What's more, we'd suffer for it
    If she, the wretch, learnt that Orestes is alive.

PEASANT: Well, if you think it best, I'll go to the old man
    And take your message. You go in now straight away
    And get things ready. When a woman's put to it
    She can find odds and ends to make a meal look good.
    Well, surely there's at least enough left in the house
    To stuff their guts for one day? – When I find myself
    Frustrated in such matters, I think, 'What a power
    There is in money! You can entertain a guest;
    Or, if you're ill, buy medicine and cure yourself.'
    For the rest – well, each day's eating doesn't come to much.
    Rich bellies hold about the same amount as poor.

       Exeunt ELECTRA *and* PEASANT *severally*.

CHORUS:
    Famous were the ships
    Which sailed long ago from Hellas to Troy,
    When the dancing of oars without number
    Joined in their journey the dancing sea-nymphs,
    Where, drawn by the music of flutes,
    Dolphins were leaping and rolling
    Beside the purple-painted prows,
    Bearing on his way the son of Thetis,

The light-footed leaper Achilles,
Who went with Agamemnon's army
To the rocky Trojan coast and the Simois river.

Passing the headlands of Euboea
The Nereids came, carrying
Golden armour for a prince of fighters,
The labour of Hephaestus' forge,
To the slopes of Mount Pelion,
To the holy glens of precipitous Ossa,
The high haunts of mountain-nymphs,
Seeking Achilles the young runner,
Grandson of the salt sea,
Where for the sake of the sons of Atreus
The old Centaur was rearing him
As a light of hope for Hellas.

I heard a man from Troy describing,
As he stood in the harbour at Nauplia,
Your famous shield, son of Thetis,
Engraved all round with figures
Which terrified the Trojans:
On the outermost rim was Perseus
Hovering on winged sandals over the sea,
Holding the severed head of the dread Gorgon,
And with him Hermes, Zeus's messenger,
The son of Maia, god of country places.

In the centre of the shield blazed forth
The gleaming circle of the sun
Drawn by winged horses,
And the celestial dancing constellations,
The Pleiads and the Hyades,
Which Hector saw, and fled;
And on the helmet of beaten gold

Were Sphinxes, their claws clutching
The prey caught by their enchantments;
And on the rounded corselet
That lioness breathing fire,
Her clawed feet stretched in flight
At the sight of Pegasus the horse of Pyrene.

And on Achilles' deadly sword appeared
Four prancing horses harnessed together,
And the dust rose dark around their flanks.
Such were the warriors whose commander
Your adultery sent to his death,
Evil-hearted daughter of Tyndareos!
Therefore you too the heavenly gods will send to death;
The day will come when I shall see
The steel blade set to your throat
And your life pour forth in blood.

Enter an OLD MAN *carrying various provisions.*

OLD MAN: Where's my young mistress? Where's Electra,
    my princess,
  Whose father Agamemnon I brought up? – Oh, dear!
  This path up to her house is far too steep for me,
  A wrinkled old man. Still, a friend's a friend; so I
  Must drag myself up – bent back, wobbly knee, and all.

        [ELECTRA *appears at the door.*]

  Ah, there you are! My daughter! Look, I've brought you a
    lamb
  Bred in my own flock; quite young – took it from the ewe
  This morning; and some flowers; and cheese, straight from
    the press.
  And here's a little of Dionysus' treasure – old,
  Rich-scented; it's not much – but pour a cup of this
  Into your weaker wine, to give it body. There!
  Let someone take all this in to your guests. My eyes
  Are full of tears, I must just wipe them on my old coat.

121

ELECTRA: Why do you weep, old man? It can't be *my* con-
    dition,
  My grief that stirs your memory after all this time?
  Or does the thought of Orestes' exile make you sad?
  Or do you mourn my father, whom your care brought
    up –
  Though you and those you love see no reward for it?
OLD MAN: No, no reward. But there's one thing I would
    not bear:
  On my way here I passed his grave. I was alone.
  I knelt down, and shed tears; and then I opened this
  Wineskin I brought for your two guests, and poured some
    wine
  There as an offering, and spread some myrtle-branches
  Over the grave. And there, right on the altar, lay
  A black-fleeced ewe just newly sacrificed – the blood
  Still wet; and near it a lock of dark brown hair, cut off.
  I wonder, now, who it could be? What man would dare
  To visit that grave? Certainly no Argive would.
  Perhaps – perhaps your brother came there secretly
  And paid this reverence to his father's desolate tomb.
  Go there yourself, and put that hair against your own;
  See if their colour tallies. Children of one father
  Often have many features that are similar.
ELECTRA: You should know better than to think that *my*
    brother,
  My brave Orestes, would have come here secretly
  Because he feared Aegisthus. Anyway, how could
  The two locks correspond, the one a nobleman's,
  Grown like an athlete's in the palaestra, mine a woman's,
  Softened with combing? It's absurd. Besides, you'd find
  Many with similar hair, who are not of the same blood.
OLD MAN: Then go and try the shoe-prints there with your
    own foot,
  My child; see if the shape and size are like your own.

ELECTRA: Foot-prints? How could there be foot-prints on
　　rocky ground?

　　And if there could, brother's and sister's feet would not

　　Be the same size; the weaker sex has smaller feet.

OLD MAN: That's true: if he *has* come, we can't be sure of it.

　　Yet, should you meet him face to face, would he not wear,

　　For recognition, the cloak, woven on your loom, in which

　　Long ago, to save his life, I smuggled him away?

ELECTRA: Surely you know that, when Orestes went away,

　　I was a child? Even if I had been weaving clothes,

　　Clothes don't grow larger on the body; he wouldn't now

　　Be wearing the same cloak he had in infancy.

　　No; either a stranger pitied the neglected grave

　　And laid a lock there; or some Argive dared to elude

　　The guards, and make dutiful offerings to the dead.

OLD MAN: But where are your two guests? I want to see
　　them now

　　And question them about your brother.

ELECTRA: 　　　　　　　　　　　　Here they come.

　　ORESTES *and* PYLADES *come briskly out of the cottage.*

OLD MAN [*aside*]: They have nobility; but it may be counter-
　　feit.

　　Many that are nobly born belie it. None the less –

　　[*to Orestes and Pylades*] My courteous greeting to our guests.

ORESTES: 　　　　　　　　　　　　Greeting, old man.

　　– Electra, whose friend is this antique relic here?

ELECTRA: This man, Sir, was my father's guardian when a
　　child.

ORESTES: What? The same man who got your brother safely
　　away?

ELECTRA: Yes; if Orestes lives, he owes his life to him.

ORESTES: Well . . .?

　　Why does he stare at me, like a man examining

　　The head on a new silver coin? Perhaps he thinks

　　I am like someone.

ELECTRA: You are one of Orestes' friends;
He is glad to see you.

ORESTES: Yes, Orestes is my friend. —
Why is he walking round me?

ELECTRA: I am wondering too.

OLD MAN: My daughter, royal Electra! Pray to the great
gods —

ELECTRA: What shall I pray for — of all things in heaven and
earth?

OLD MAN: To grasp the precious treasure God reveals to
you.

ELECTRA: Very well; I call upon the gods. — What do you
mean?

OLD MAN: Look at this man, my child. There's no one you
love more.

ELECTRA: I have been looking — to see if you have lost your
wits.

OLD MAN: Lost my wits? When I see your brother before
my eyes?

ELECTRA: My brother? No! I can't believe it.

OLD MAN: You are looking
At Agamemnon's son, Orestes.

ELECTRA: Do you see
Some token, to convince me?

OLD MAN: This scar on his brow;
He fell and cut it once at home, chasing a fawn
With you.

ELECTRA: What's that? A scar? I see it, yes —

OLD MAN·   Then why
Hesitate? He's your brother: take him in your arms!

ELECTRA: I will! Your tokens have convinced me. — O my
brother!

[*They embrace.*]

I thought you'd never come. At last I hold you close.

ORESTES: At last you are in my arms.

124

ELECTRA: I had despaired.

ORESTES: I too.

ELECTRA: You really are Orestes?

ORESTES: Yes; your one ally.
   And if I catch the prey I've come to hunt –

ELECTRA: You will!
   I am certain. We can never again believe in gods
   If wickedness is now to triumph over right.

CHORUS:
> It has come, at last it has come!
> The bright day has dawned;
> Our deliverer stands before us,
> A beacon of hope for Argos;
> Who far from his father's house
> Lived so many years a homeless exile.
> God is with us, Electra;
> God leads us in our turn to victory.
> Lift your hands, lift your voice,
> Pour your prayer to the gods
> That with good success your brother
> May enter the gates of Argos.

ORESTES: Enough, sister; this mutual meeting and embrace
   Is a dear pleasure, which in time we will renew.
   Now tell me, old man – your coming is a lucky chance –
   I am here for vengeance on my father's murderer
   And on my mother, his partner both in crime and lust:
   What is my next step? Have I any friends in Argos?
   Or am I bankrupt – as in fortune, so in all?
   Whom shall I contact? Shall I go by night or day?
   What way shall I set out to meet my enemies?

OLD MAN: My son, you are an exile: you have not one
   friend.
   It's a rare piece of fortune if a man will share
   Both good and bad with you. In your friends' eyes you are
   Uprooted, finished; no one pins his hopes on you.

Listen: success lies in your luck and your strong arm,
If you're to get back Argos and your father's house.

ORESTES: Yes, that's my aim. What must I do to reach it?

OLD MAN: Kill
Aegisthus and your mother.

ORESTES: That's the glorious deed
I've come to attempt. But how achieve it?

OLD MAN: It's no use
To think of getting inside the walls.

ORESTES: Aegisthus has,
I take it, guards and sentries everywhere?

OLD MAN: You're right.
He's afraid of you; he can't sleep.

ORESTES: What do you suggest?

OLD MAN: Well, listen now; I've thought of something.

ORESTES: May it be
A good proposal, and may I understand it right.

OLD MAN: On my way here I saw Aegisthus.

ORESTES: Splendid: where?

OLD MAN: Not far off, in the pastures where his horses graze.

ORESTES: What was he doing? This may solve the insoluble.

OLD MAN: Preparing a banquet for the Nymphs – or so it
seemed.

ORESTES: As thanks for children, or vows for an expected
birth?

OLD MAN: He had everything in hand to sacrifice a bull,
That's all I know.

ORESTES: How many men were with him? Or
Had he just slaves?

OLD MAN: Some of his household staff were there;
No Argives.

ORESTES: Might there be some who would recognize me?

OLD MAN: They're slaves; they never saw you.

ORESTES: Suppose I kill the man –
Would they be friendly?

OLD MAN: Slaves will always serve success;
That's in your favour.

ORESTES: How should I best get close to him?

OLD MAN: Go and stand where he'll see you at the sacrifice.

ORESTES: You mean, his land lies close along the road?

OLD MAN: Why, yes;
He'll see you, and invite you in to share the feast.

ORESTES: By the gods' help, he'll find me an unwelcome
guest.

OLD MAN: From then on you must make your plans as things
turn out.

ORESTES: You're right. Where is my mother?

OLD MAN: She's in Argos still;
But she'll be with her husband for the festival.

ORESTES: Why did she not start out with him?

OLD MAN: Why, she's afraid
Of harsh words from the people; so she stayed behind.

ORESTES: I well believe it; she knows what they think of
her.

OLD MAN: That's so; she's hated by them as a woman
accursed.

ORESTES: Well, then: am I to kill them both at the same time?

ELECTRA: The killing of my mother I shall claim myself.

ORESTES: Good; and in *my* part I'll take Fortune for my
guide.

ELECTRA: And this old friend will help us in our separate
tasks.

OLD MAN: I will. What plan have you for Clytemnestra's
death?

ELECTRA: This: go and tell her I have borne a child – a son.

OLD MAN: Shall I say this was recent, or some time ago?

ELECTRA: Ten days ago, say; that gives time for purifying.

OLD MAN: And how is this to bring about your mother's
death?

ELECTRA: When she is told of my confinement she will come.

OLD MAN: Will she? You think, daughter, she cares for you
at all?

ELECTRA: Yes; she will come and weep over my son's low
birth.

OLD MAN: Perhaps; but bring your argument back to the
point.

ELECTRA: Once here, the rest is simple: she's as good as
dead.

OLD MAN: But even suppose she comes here – comes right
to your door –?

ELECTRA: Surely from here it's just a short by-path to death?

OLD MAN: Let me once see this done, and I can die content.

ELECTRA: But first, now, you must show my brother where
to go

To find Aegisthus.

OLD MAN: Yes, at the sacrifice.

ELECTRA: – And then

Go on to meet my mother and tell her what I said.

OLD MAN: Your very words – she'll think you're telling her
yourself.

ELECTRA: Orestes, now to work. You draw first blood.

ORESTES: I'm ready,

Given a guide.

OLD MAN: I'll take you there most willingly.

They all raise their hands in prayer.

ORESTES: Zeus! Conqueror of my father's enemies and mine!

ELECTRA: Have pity on us; for our state is pitiable.

OLD MAN: Have pity on them: they are yours by birth and
blood.

ELECTRA: Hera, great Queen, to whom Mycenae's altars
burn!

ORESTES: If these our prayers are just, O grant us victory.

OLD MAN: O grant them a just vengeance for their father's
death.

They kneel.

ORESTES: My father, sent by foul crime to your home below!

ELECTRA: And Earth, great Sovreign, whom my beating hands invoke!

OLD MAN: Send now to these dear children strong defence and aid.

ORESTES: Bring the whole army of the dead to fight your cause.

ELECTRA: Bring all the brave who shared your victory over Troy.

OLD MAN: Bring all who hate impure hearts and polluted hands.

A pause. ORESTES *and the* OLD MAN *rise.*

ELECTRA: Father, so outraged by my mother! Do you hear?

OLD MAN: He has heard all, I am certain. – It is time to go.

ELECTRA *rises.*

ELECTRA: I give you then this token-word: 'Aegisthus dies.'
  If in the struggle you are thrown and lose your life,
  Be sure I shall not live: that moment is my death.
  I'll drive a sword into my heart.

ORESTES: I understand.

ELECTRA: Then take your courage in both hands.
  [*Exeunt* ORESTES, PYLADES, OLD MAN, *and Attendants.*]
                                        Women! Your part
  Will be, like beacons after battle, to raise the cry
  For life or death. I'll be on watch; and my hand too
  Will hold a sword. If I'm defeated, my enemies
  Shall never glut their vengeance on my living flesh.

Exit ELECTRA.

CHORUS:
     Long ago, in the mountains of Argos,
     A soft young lamb under its ewe
     (So say the grey-haired spinners of old tales)
     Was found by Pan, prince of wild places,
     Who breathes enchanting music on his tuned reeds;
     And the lamb had a lovely fleece of pure gold.

And Pan, they say, brought it to Atreus king of Argos;
And there a herald stood on the marble steps, and cried,
'People of Mycenae, come all, come all!
Come and see this wonderful sight,
Our great king's treasure.'
And the people came at once
And honoured the royal palace with dancing and singing.

And braziers of beaten gold were placed about;
And all over the city of Argos
Fire gleamed on the altars;
And the flute, servant of the Muses,
Sounded forth its sweet notes,
And lovely songs rose loud
In praise of the golden lamb.
Then Thyestes turned to treachery.
He lay secretly with Atreus' wife,
And persuaded her;
And he took the marvellous lamb to his own house.
Then going forth to the assembled people he proclaimed
That he held in his own house the horned marvel,
The lamb with the golden fleece.

Then, then it was that Zeus turned back
The glittering journeys of the stars
And the burning sun and the pale face of dawn;
And from that day on, the blaze of divine fire
Drives always towards the western sky;
And the wet clouds lie to the north,
And the parched plains of Ammon languish untouched by
    dew,
And Zeus witholds from them his sweet rain.

That is the story. But I can hardly believe
That the golden sun turned his face,

Changed his burning course,
To help a mortal's misfortune
And requite a human sin.
Nevertheless, frightening tales are useful:
They promote reverence for the gods.
O Clytemnestra, sister of two famous brothers!
Had you but remembered tales like these
As you raised your hand to kill your husband!

CHORUS: Ah!
  Friends, what was that? Did I imagine it – a shout
  Like subterranean thunder? Or did you hear it too?
  The gale is up, I tell you, and brings news. – My lady!
  Electra! Come out here!

Enter ELECTRA.

ELECTRA: What is it? The fight is on –
Where do we stand?

CHORUS: I heard a cry, like death. That's all.

ELECTRA: I heard a cry too; at some distance, but I heard.

CHORUS [*still listening*]: The sound comes from far off, but
    unmistakable.

ELECTRA: That was an Argive voice – a groan. Was it my
    brother?

CHORUS: I can't tell. There's a chorus now of mingled cries.

ELECTRA: That means the sword for me – now; I must lose no
    time.

CHORUS: No! Wait at least until you know the worst is
    true.

ELECTRA: I must not. We have lost. There would be news by
    now.

CHORUS: There will be. It's no easy matter to kill a king.

Enter a MESSENGER.

MESSENGER: Victory, women of Mycenae! Victory!
  To all friends I proclaim Orestes' victory!
  Aegisthus, Agamemnon's murderer, lies dead.
  Thanks be to all the gods!

ELECTRA: Who are you? How do I know
Your news is true?

MESSENGER: You know me – I'm your brother's servant!

ELECTRA: Dear friend, forgive me. Terror made me blind;
    but now
I recognize you well enough. Tell me again:
The loathsome wretch who killed my father – is he dead?

MESSENGER: He's dead. Good news twice told is twice wel-
    come to you.

ELECTRA: O gods, and Justice, who behold all things! At last
You have come! – Friend, tell me point by point about this
    death.
My brother killed Thyestes' son: how? I must know.

MESSENGER: After we left this cottage, we soon reached a
    road
Wide enough for two wagons; and we followed this
To where the great king of Mycenae was. He stood
In a well-watered plot, cutting young myrtle-leaves
To make a garland for his head. When he saw us
He called out, 'Greeting, strangers! Who are you? And
    where
Do you come from? What's your country?' And Orestes said,
'We are Thessalians, and we're going to the Alpheius
To sacrifice to Olympian Zeus.' When he heard that
Aegisthus said, 'Stay here today and be my guests.
I'm killing a bull in honour of the Nymphs; and you
Must share the banquet. Get up in good time tomorrow –
You'll be there just as soon. Come on, into the house.'
And as he said this he was leading us by the hand –
'I won't let you refuse,' he cried. 'Here, one of you,
Bring water for these guests to wash; and let them stand
Close to the altar, by the purifying bowl.'

Orestes answered, 'We have purified ourselves
Just now, in holy water from a running stream.

132

So, King Aegisthus, if strangers may lawfully
Join in the sacrifice with Argives, we will not
Refuse your bidding; here we are.' That settled that.
The slaves guarding the king laid by their spears; and all
At once were busy: some held baskets; others brought
The sacrificial bowl; others again lit fires
And put pots on to boil; and the whole house was full
Of noise and movement.

                Then your mother's lover took
Barley, and threw it on the altar, with these words:
'Nymphs of these rocks, I pray that many times both I
And my dear wife at home may offer sacrifice
With the same fortune we enjoy today; and may
Evil oppress my enemies' – by which he meant
You and Orestes. Then under his breath my master
Prayed contrary, to possess again his father's house.
Aegisthus from the basket took the straight-edged blade,
And cut from the beast's head one tuft; with his right hand
He placed this on the holy flame; then, as the slaves
Lifted the young bull shoulder-high, he cut its throat;
Then said to Orestes:

'I've heard it boasted that Thessalians are expert
At two things: cutting up a dead bull skilfully,
And breaking horses to the rein. Friend, here's the sword:
Show us now if that's true about Thessalians.'

It was a well-made Dorian sword. He grasped it firm,
Threw off his buckled cloak, called Pylades to help,
Made all the slaves stand back; then took the bull-calf's leg,
And with one long sweep laid the pale flesh bare, and
    flayed
The carcase in less time than a fast runner takes
To run a mile; then opened up the guts. At once

Aegisthus took the augural parts and gazed at them.
The liver-lobe was missing; and the portal-vein
And gall-bladder portended evil visitations
To one that saw them. The king's face grew dark. Orestes
Asked him, 'What has upset you?' 'Friend, I'm much in
    fear,'
He said, 'of treachery from abroad. Agamemnon's son,
Of all men living, is the most dangerous enemy
To me and to my royal house.' Orestes said,
'What? You, king of a city, fear an exile's plots?'
This Dorian knife's too small; bring me a Phthian sword;
I'll split the breast-bone, then we can fall to and feast.'

They brought one, and he cut. Aegisthus took the parts
To separate them, bending over them. Orestes
Rose on his toes, and struck him on the joint of the neck,
Shattering his spine. His whole body from head to foot
Writhed, shuddered in death-agony. The king's guards ran
And seized their spears – a whole regiment against two.
They stood their ground and faced them boldly. Orestes
    cried,
'I am no enemy to Argos, nor to you,
My comrades. This man was my father's murderer,
Whom I have punished – I am Orestes. You were once
My father's servants: will you take my life?' At this
They checked their spears; in a moment he was recognized
By an old man who had long served the royal house.
And there they were, cheering and shouting with delight,
And putting garlands on him. Now he's coming here,
Bringing no Gorgon's head to show you, but the head
Of your enemy, Aegisthus. His atrocious debt
Has fallen due; his life at last pays blood for blood.

CHORUS:

    Oh, Electra! Set your feet dancing!
    Dance like a light fawn

That springs in rapture heaven-high!
Orestes has achieved his task
And won a crown more glorious than the Olympic crown.
Come, match our dancing with your victory song.

ELECTRA: O holy light! O glorious chariot of the sun!
O earth! O night, that till this moment filled my eyes!
Now all is freedom, eyes may open unafraid:
Aegisthus lies dead, who destroyed my father's life.
Come, friends; such festive finery as I still possess
Stored in the house, I must bring out, to crown with joy
My brother's head, and celebrate his victory.

Exit ELECTRA *to the cottage.*

CHORUS:
Go, then, bring the crown for his head;
We meanwhile will dance to delight the Muses.
Now our own true king,
Of the line that we loved in the old days,
Has destroyed the usurper
And holds his rightful rule in Argos.
Come, let heart and voice rise together.

ELECTRA *returns carrying two crowns or wreaths, as* ORESTES
enters with PYLADES, *followed by others bearing the body of*
AEGISTHUS.

ELECTRA: Welcome, brave conqueror! Welcome, Orestes,
worthy son
Of him who conquered Troy! Come, let me bind your hair
With this triumphal crown. You have run your full course
And come home bearing your just prize – your enemy
Dead at your feet, who struck down your father and mine.
– You too, receive from me this garland, Pylades,
His brave comrade-in-arms, son of an honourable man.
You have shared equally with him in this ordeal;
I pray for both of you a long and happy life.

ORESTES: Name first the gods, Electra, as accomplishers
Of this good fortune; give your second place of praise

To me, who am the gods' and Fortune's instrument.
I have in full truth killed Aegisthus. So that knowledge
May be confirmed by visible truth, here is himself.

[*He shows the head of Aegisthus.*]

Do what you wish; throw out his carcase to the dogs,
Impale him on a stake, to feed the birds of heaven.
He's yours, Electra; once your master, now your slave.

ELECTRA: Shame makes me shrink from words which my will
    prompts me to.

ORESTES: What shame? There's nothing you need fear.

ELECTRA: Shame makes me fear
    To insult the dead, lest sharp resentment point at me.

ORESTES: No one would blame you.

ELECTRA: Our citizens are quick to blame
    And hard to please.

ORESTES: Say what you wish, sister. The feud
    We had with this dead man was unconditional.

ELECTRA: Of all the harsh and bitter things I have to say,
    What shall come first, what last? and what shall come
        between?
    For years I have never failed at sunrise to say over
    All that I longed to tell you to your face, if ever
    I left behind that terror-ridden past. And now
    I am free. I'll pay off now those evil words which I
    Wanted to say to you when you were still alive.

    You were the ruin of my life. I and my brother
    Did you no wrong; but you made us both fatherless.
    Adulterously you took my mother; then you killed
    Her husband, chief commander of the Greeks – though you
    Yourself never saw Troy. Then, you were such a fool
    As to imagine, when you had shamed my father's bed,
    That in my mother you would find a faithful wife.
    When an adulterer corrupts his neighbour's wife,
    And then is forced to marry her, let him be sure

136

Of this: he's to be pitied if he dreams that she,
Who cuckolded one husband, will not cuckold two.
It was a sorry life you lived, though unaware:
You knew your marriage was unholy; and she knew
Her husband was an enemy of the gods; so each,
Being evil, gained the other's evil destiny,
She yours, you hers. And no Argive called her your wife;
But always 'Clytemnestra's husband' was your name.

Is it not shameful, when the wife, and not the husband,
Takes the first place at home? So too when boys are known
Not as their father's sons, but as their mother's – that
Is something which I hate. For when a man has married
A noble wife above his station, not a word
Is said about him; all the talk is of his wife.

What more than all deluded your dull mind was this:
You thought that having great wealth made you a great man.
But money keeps you company a little while;
What's firm and lasting is man's nature, not his wealth.
A noble nature is a lifelong friend, and lifts
Life's burdens; wealth makes unjust league with wickedness,
And, flowering a brief season, soon flies out of doors.

As for your way with women, since plain speech does not
Become a virgin, I'll pick words discreetly. You,
Equipped with both a royal palace and good looks,
Indulged. . . . Give me for husband not a girl-faced fop,
But a true man, whose sons devote themselves to arms.
The other sort shine at a dance, and nowhere else.

Then perish, ignorant how the ripe years have condemned
Your guilt! – Let no man, deep in wickedness like his,
Think, if at first his stride is strong, he can outstrip
Justice, till he has run his race and come safe home.

CHORUS: His crimes were fearful; and he has paid a fearful price

To both of you. Justice is irresistible.

ELECTRA: Men, take his body in and put it out of sight.

My mother must not see it before her throat is cut.

O RESTES *sees* CLYTEMNESTRA *approaching some way off.*

ORESTES: Wait. There are other things we must decide.

ELECTRA [*looking in the same direction*]: What is it?

An armed force from Mycenae?

ORESTES: No. It is my mother.

ELECTRA: Good: she is stepping straight into the trap. – Why, look!

How fine she is – a carriage, slaves, and her best gown!

ORESTES: What shall we do, then? Are we going to kill our mother?

ELECTRA: Have you grown soft, as soon as you set eyes on her?

ORESTES: She brought me up, she bore me! How can I take her life?

ELECTRA: How? As she took our father Agamemnon's life.

ORESTES: Phoebus, your oracle is blind brutality!

ELECTRA: Whose eyes can hope to see, then, if Apollo's blind?

ORESTES: It is wrong to kill my mother! Yet you said I must.

ELECTRA: You avenge your father – what harm comes to you from that?

ORESTES: Avenging him I am pure; but killing her, condemned.

ELECTRA: If you neglect to avenge him you defy the gods.

ORESTES: But if I kill my mother, shall I not be punished?

ELECTRA: *He* will pursue you, if you let his vengeance go.

ORESTES: Some fiend disguised as god commanded me.

ELECTRA: A fiend –

Throned on the holy tripod? Most improbable.

ORESTES: I can't believe that what the god told me is right.

138

ELECTRA: You're not to lose your nerve and play the coward now.

> You're going to use the same deception that *she* used
> When with Aegisthus' help she struck her husband down.

ORESTES: I'll go in. Every step is dreadful; and the deed
Before me, still more dreadful. Yet, if Heaven so wills,
Let it be done. Heaven cannot help my agony.

> *Exeunt* ORESTES *and* PYLADES *into the house.*
> *Enter* CLYTEMNESTRA *attended by female slaves.*

CHORUS:

> Daughter of Tyndareos,
> Queen of the land of Argos,
> Sister of the two noble sons of Zeus
> Who live among stars in the fiery heaven
> And are honoured on stormy seas
> As saviours of men's lives:
> Greeting, Lady.
> For your great wealth and prosperity
> We worship you as one of the blessed gods.
> We have waited long for this happy day;
> Much will be put right by your coming.
> Welcome, Queen.

CLYTEMNESTRA: Get out of the carriage, Trojan slaves. Now take my hand

And help me to the ground. – The spoils of Troy adorn
Our holy temples; these, the choicest of Troy's women,
Are mine – small compensation for the child I lost;
Still, they look lovely in my palace.

ELECTRA: Why should not I
Be given this privilege, to hold your royal hand?
I am a slave too, banished from my father's house
To misery.

CLYTEMNESTRA: I have my slaves here; pray don't trouble.

ELECTRA: You took me prisoner by the sword, uprooted me.

Was I not, like them, captured in a conquered palace?
Like them, am I not fatherless?
CLYTEMNESTRA: Your father, child,
Brought all this on you by his wicked treachery
To one he should have loved. Listen: I know my tongue
Is sometimes bitter; that's because I'm spoken of
As a bad woman. I agree, one should not speak
Bitterly. But when people judge someone, they ought
To learn the facts, and then hate, if they've reason to.
And if they find no reason, then they should not hate.

When I married your father, I did not expect
To die, or see my children killed. He took my child
To Aulis, where the fleet lay bound; lured her from home
With lies about Achilles; held her high above
The altar; then her father cut her soft white throat –
My Iphigenia. If he had done it to avert
The capture of his city, or to exalt his house;
Or if, to save his other children, he had taken
One life for many, he could be forgiven. But no:
Helen was a whore, her husband didn't know how to handle
A randy wife; and *that* was Agamemnon's reason
For murdering my daughter. All the same, for that –
Wicked as it was – I would not have turned savage, or
Have killed my husband. But he must bring home with him
The mad prophetess; foist on me a second wife,
A fellow-lodger – two kept women in one house.

Well, women are frail, I grant you. But when, knowing this,
A husband looks elsewhere, and slights his lawful wife,
She'll copy him, and find herself another friend.
And then the glare of public censure lights on *us*;
The husbands are to blame – but they're not criticized.
Suppose Menelaus had been abducted secretly,
Would I have had to kill Orestes, to get back

My sister's husband Menelaus? Would your father
Have stood for that? No: he'd have killed me if I'd touched
His son; he killed my daughter – why should he not die?
I killed him. I took the only way open to me –
Turned for help to his enemies. Well, what could I do?
None of your father's friends would have helped me murder
    him.

So, if you're anxious to refute me, do it now;
Speak freely; prove your father's death not justified.

CHORUS: Your words are just; yet in your 'justice' there
    remains
Something repellent. A wife ought in all things to accept
Her husband's judgement, if she is wise. Those who will not
Admit this, fall outside my scope of argument.

ELECTRA: Mother, remember what you said just now. You
    promised
That I might state my opinion freely without fear.

CLYTEMNESTRA: I said so, daughter, and I meant it.

ELECTRA: Do you mean
You'll listen first, and get your own back afterwards?

CLYTEMNESTRA: No, no; you're free to say what your heart
    wants to say.

ELECTRA: I'll say it, then. This is where I'll begin. I wish,
Mother, your heart were purer. You and Helen both
Were rightly praised for beauty; but unhappily
In heart too you are sisters, both lascivious.
Castor must blush for you. They talk of Helen's 'rape' –
She embraced her own corruption! You destroyed the life
Of the most noble man in Hellas – your pretext,
That you avenged your daughter with your husband's blood.
There may be some believe you; but I know you well.

Before your daughter's sacrifice was decided on,
When Agamemnon still was scarcely out of sight,

You were before your mirror, smoothing out your hair.
A wife who in her husband's absence will take pains
To enhance her beauty, may be written off as bad.
She has no need to show a pretty face outdoors
Unless she's seeking what she should not. You alone
Of all Greek women – as I know – if ever Troy
Gained some success, were happy; if Troy lost a battle
Your eyes were clouded. Why? Because you didn't want
Agamemnon to come back from Troy. And yet you had
Every inducement to be faithful. Agamemnon
Was not inferior to Aegisthus in descent;
A man whom Hellas chose for her Commander-in-chief.
Further, when Helen your sister so disgraced herself,
You had a chance to make your name; for wickedness
Acts as a foil to virtue and makes it noticeable.

This next: if, as you say, my father killed your daughter,
What injury have I and my brother done to you?
Why, after you had killed your husband, did you not
Make over to us our father's house? Instead you took
As dowry to your lover what was not your own,
And bought yourself a husband. Aegisthus does not
Suffer exile in payment for Orestes' wrongs,
Nor death for mine, though he inflicts a living death
On me, far crueller than my sister's. And if death
In justice demands death, why, then, I and your son
Orestes must kill you to avenge our father's death;
For if the one revenge is just, so is the other.

CLYTEMNESTRA: My child, your nature has always been to
    love your father.
It is natural; some children love their fathers best,
And some their mothers. I'll forgive you. I do not,
In fact, exult unduly over what I did.
With what insensate fury I drove myself to take
My grand revenge! How bitterly I regret it now!

ELECTRA: It's too late for regret; you can't undo what's done.
Well, though my father's dead, your son Orestes lives,
Exiled from Argos. Why do you not bring him home?

CLYTEMNESTRA: Because I'm terrified; not for him, but for
myself.
They say he is full of anger for his father's death.

ELECTRA: Why do you let Aegisthus still persecute *me*?

CLYTEMNESTRA: You know his temper. Yours too is im-
placable.

ELECTRA: I have good reason; but I'll put my anger aside.

CLYTEMNESTRA: Do; and you'll find he will stop persecuting
you.

ELECTRA: He lives in my house; and that makes him arrogant.

CLYTEMNESTRA: There you go, kindling the old quarrel
once again.

ELECTRA: I'll keep quiet. I'm afraid of him – so much afraid.

CLYTEMNESTRA: Let's change the subject. Child, why did
you send for me?

ELECTRA: You were told of my confinement, were you not?

CLYTEMNESTRA: I was.
But why are you in this state – so dirty, so ill-dressed?
The birth's well over now.

ELECTRA: Will you do this for me? –
Offer the customary tenth-day sacrifice
For a son. I've never had a child before, so I'm
No expert in these matters.

CLYTEMNESTRA: It is usually done
By the woman who delivered you.

ELECTRA: I was alone.
I delivered myself.

CLYTEMNESTRA: What? Is this house so far
From any neighbour?

ELECTRA: We are poor; we don't have friends.

CLYTEMNESTRA: Well, as a favour, I'll go in, and pay the
gods

The proper dues for your son. And then I must be off
To where my husband's sacrificing to the Nymphs
Out in the pasture. [*To her servants*] – You, there! take the
  carriage away
And feed the horses. Give me as much time as I need
To make this offering to the gods; then come for me.
[*To Electra*] I have my husband too to think of.

ELECTRA: Please come in
To our poor house. Take care this smoky wall does not
Dirty your dress. Now you shall offer to the gods
The sacrifice that is due.

               [CLYTEMNESTRA *goes in.*]
                    All is prepared. The sword
Of sacrifice which felled the bull, by whose side you
Shall fall, is sharpened for you. In the house of Death
You shall be still his bride whose bed you shared in life.
This 'favour' is all I grant you. In return I take
Justice, your life in payment for my father's life.

               ELECTRA *goes in.*

CHORUS:
    Now retribution follows sin;
    Through the fated house a new wind blows.
    Long ago my beloved lord and king
    Fell dead by the water of purification;
    And through the rooms, round the stone cornice,
    Rang out his death-cry,
    'O wicked, wretched wife, why will you murder me,
    Returned after ten harvests
    Home to my own country?'

    Now like a returning tide
    Justice arraigns the reckless adulteress
    Who, when her husband after many years
    Came home to his heaven-high Cyclopean fortress,
    Grasped the whetted axe,

With her own hand struck and felled him.
Pity the victim of her vengeance,
Whatever raging wrongs possessed her.
Like a lioness from the mountains
Roaming through meadows and orchards,
She carried out her purpose.

CLYTEMNESTRA [*within*]: My children, for the gods' sake,
don't kill your mother!

CHORUS: Do you hear that shriek in the house?

CLYTEMNESTRA: Help! Oh, oh!

CHORUS 1:
She calls for pity, and I pity her,
Done to death by her own children.

CHORUS 2:
Soon or late, Heaven dispenses justice.
Poor, desperate queen, your suffering was bitter;
But your revenge on your husband was unholy.

CHORUS: They are coming, clothed in fresh streams of their
mother's blood –
Trophy of triumph over that beseeching cry.
There is no other house, nor ever was, whose fate
More rends the heart, than the great house of Tantalus.

Enter ORESTES *and* ELECTRA, *both overcome with horror.*
Attendants bring the body of Clytemnestra.

ORESTES:
O Earth!
O Zeus, whose eye sees everything men do:
Look at this!
This bloody, abominable sight!
Two bodies lying together on the ground –
And my hand struck them down,
To avenge wrong done to me!
Where can I find tears enough?

ELECTRA:
Tears, my brother – let tears be endless.

I am guilty.
I was burning with desperate rage against her;
Yet she was my mother, I her daughter.

CHORUS 1:

How terrible was your fate,
Mother of curses!
Now with doubled anguish
The curses you bore have turned upon you.

CHORUS 2:

Yet, since you killed their father,
Their revenge is just.

ORESTES:

O Phoebus, in the command of your oracle
Justice was hidden from me;
But in its fulfilment
You have made torment clear.
You have bestowed on me, for my obedience,
A murderer's destiny, far from Hellas.
To what city shall I go?
Will any friend, will any man who fears God,
Dare to look in my face –
A son who has killed his mother?

ELECTRA:

Oh, what shall I do?
Where shall I go?
What happy company will welcome me
To a dance or a wedding?
What man will accept me as his wife?

CHORUS:

Your mind has returned to itself,
And blows now with the wind of truth.
Now your thoughts are holy;
But then they defied the gods.
Dear Electra, you did a dreadful wrong to your brother,
Forcing him against his will.

ORESTES:

> Did you see how, in her agony,
> She opened her gown, thrust forth her breast,
> And showed it to me as I struck?
> Her body that gave me birth
> Sprawled there on the ground.
> I had her by the hair . . .

CHORUS:

> I know what torture you went through;
> I heard her shriek – your own mother.

ELECTRA:

> Yes; as she uttered that shriek
> She was putting her hand on my face;
> 'My child, I implore you,' she said.
> Then she hung around my neck
> So that the sword fell out of my hand.

CHORUS:

> Wretched, miserable woman! How could you bear
> To see with your own eyes
> Your mother gasping out her life?

ORESTES:

> I held my cloak over my eyes,
> While with my sword I performed sacrifice,
> Driving the blade into my mother's throat.

ELECTRA:

> And I urged you on,
> And held the sword, my hand beside yours.

CHORUS:

> Could any act be more dreadful?

ORESTES:

> Come, help me to cover her limbs with her dress;
> And close her wounds.
> – You were mother to your murderers.

ELECTRA:

> As we wrap this cloak round you

147

We love you, though we hated you.

CHORUS:

This the appointed end of great sorrows.

[*The* DIOSCORI *appear above the house.*]

Look there! Shining above the house – who are they?
Immortal spirits, or gods from heaven?
They cannot be mortals; why have they come,
Visible to our human eyes?

CASTOR: Listen, son of Agamemnon! We are the sons of
Zeus,

Your mother's brothers; I Castor, this Polydeuces.
Now, having calmed the dangerous tossing of the sea,
We have come in haste to Argos. We were witnesses;
We saw you shed our sister's, and your mother's blood.
Her fate was just; but your act is not justified.
Phoebus, yes, Phoebus – but he is my lord, so I
Am silent. He is wise; but his command to you
Was not wise. What is already done we must accept;
The future Fate and Zeus have thus ordained for you.

First, give Electra to Pylades, to have for wife.
Next, you must go from Argos; it is impossible
That you should set foot in the city, a matricide.
Moreover, those dread Fates, the dog-faced Goddesses,
Shall send you mad and drive you wandering through the
world
Till you reach Athens. There in Athene's temple cling
Fast to her holy image. She will keep at bay
Their snake-tormented fury. When Athene holds
Over your head the circle of her Gorgon-shield,
They cannot touch you. There is a place in Athens called
The Hill of Ares, where the gods once sat to cast
Their votes in the first murder-trial, when Ares, filled
With savage indignation for his daughter's rape,
Killed Halirrhothius, son of the Sea-god; a court

Where ever since, for mortal men, Justice sits firm,
Inviolable; and there you too must stand your trial
For this bloodshed. The votes being equal shall acquit you;
For Loxias, who commanded you to kill your mother,
Shall take the guilt upon himself. And this shall stand
As precedent for murder-trials in time to come,
That the accused, when votes are equal, wins his case.

The dread Goddesses, struck with grief at your acquittal,
Shall enter a deep chasm under that same hill,
Where men shall honour their abode with pious awe.
Then, you must go to Arcadia, to the river Alpheius,
And there close to the precinct of Lycean Zeus,
Settle in a city which shall take its name from you.

Such is your destiny. The dead Aegisthus here
Men of Argos shall bury in a tomb of earth.
As for your mother, Helen her sister and Menelaus
Shall bury her. They have just now reached Nauplia,
So many years since Troy was taken. Helen, in fact,
Never saw Troy; she has just come from Proteus' palace
In Egypt. Zeus sent off to Troy a phantom Helen
To stir up strife and slaughter in the human race.

Let Pylades, his virgin wife beside him, leave
This country for his home in Phocis. Let him take
With him the peasant who is your brother-in-law in name,
And make him a rich man. Orestes, you must cross
The neck of the Corinthian Isthmus, and press on
To Athens, Cecrops' city, and her god-favoured Rock.
When you have fulfilled the appointed period of blood-guilt,
You shall be quit of trouble, and find happiness.

CHORUS:
　　Sons of Zeus, is it lawful for us
　　To speak and address you?

149

CASTOR:

It is; you are not polluted with this murder.

CHORUS:

Then why did you, being gods,
And brothers of this murdered woman,
Not shield her from the pursuing vengeance?

CASTOR:

The pattern of Necessity
Led where it had to lead,
Helped by the unwise utterance of Apollo.

ORESTES:

Sons of Tyndareos, may I too speak?

CASTOR:

You may; for I lay your guilt on Apollo's shoulder.

ELECTRA:

Then what of me? No Apollo,
No oracle named *me*
As my mother's destined murderer.

CASTOR:

You shared the deed, as you share the destiny.
One fateful curse inherited from your fathers
Ravaged you both.

ORESTES:

Dear sister, after so many years
I have seen you again;
And now the love that I need from you
Is taken away.
I lose you, and you lose me.

CASTOR:

She has a husband and a home;
Her fate does not call for pity,
Except that she must leave Argos.

ELECTRA:

What grief is greater than to leave behind
The frontier of your home-land?

ORESTES:

> But I must leave my home
> To answer for my mother's blood
> Before the judgement of foreigners.

CASTOR:

> Have courage: it is the holy city of Pallas
> You are going to; so endure with patience.

ELECTRA:

> Dearest brother, embrace me;
> Let me hold you close.
> The curse of our mother's blood
> Drives us from our home,
> You one way, me another.

ORESTES:

> Fold your arms closely round me.
> Think that I am dead,
> And you mourn over my grave.

CASTOR:

> Words so charged with sorrow
> Appal the heart even of gods.
> For I too, and the greater gods of heaven,
> Feel pity for the suffering of mankind.

ORESTES:

> I shall never see you again.

ELECTRA:

> Never shall I be within sight of you.

ORESTES:

> These words are the last I shall speak to you.

ELECTRA:

> Farewell, city of Argos.
> Farewell, women of my country.

ORESTES:

> Most faithful sister, are you going now?

ELECTRA:

> I go, my eyes hot with tears.

ORESTES:

>Pylades, take Electra for your wife;
>And blessing go with you.

CASTOR [*to Orestes*]:

>Thoughts of marriage will be their comfort.
>But you must set out for Athens
>To escape these avenging hounds.
>Step by fearful step they pursue you;
>Their skin is black,
>Snakes twine round their arms;
>They bring with them fierce pains for retribution.

[*Exeunt* ORESTES *one way*, ELECTRA *and* PYLADES *another*.]

>But I and my brother speed westward, to ensure
>A safe voyage for the ships now sailing to Sicily.
>Striding through the wide plain of heaven
>We bring help – not to blasphemers,
>But to those whose life has cherished
>Goodness before god and man;
>These we deliver from their troubles,
>And bring them success.
>
>Therefore let none plot wickedness,
>Nor sail in the same ship with perjured men.
>I, a god, give this warning to mortals.

>>>>*Exeunt* DIOSCORI.

CHORUS:

>Farewell, sons of Zeus!
>
>To be able to *fare well*,
>To avoid the frustration of misfortune:
>That, in this world, is happiness.

HERACLES

*

Characters:

AMPHITRYON, *known as the father of Heracles*
MEGARA, *wife of Heracles and daughter of Creon,*
former king of Thebes
LYCUS, *usurping king of Thebes*
HERACLES, *son of Zeus and Alcmene*
IRIS, *messenger of the goddess Hera*
MADNESS
A MESSENGER
THESEUS, *king of Athens*
THREE YOUNG SONS *of Heracles*
CHORUS *of Theban Elders*

*

Scene: The forecourt of the royal palace in Thebes. Near the front of
the stage is an altar of Zeus the Deliverer; sitting grouped around
it are Amphitryon, Megara, and her three sons by Heracles.

AMPHITRYON: Is there a man living who has not heard of
   me –
Amphitryon of Argos, whose bed welcomed Zeus?
Son of Alcaeus, grandson of Perseus; and father
Of Heracles. I have lived here in Thebes ever since
The crop of Sown Men sprang full-grown out of the earth,
And Ares, of their number, spared a few, who with
Their children's children peopled Thebes. Menoeceus' son
Creon, till lately king of Thebes, was their descendant.

This is Megara, Creon's daughter. Long ago
Among the assembled Thebans wedding-music rose
From voice and flute, when the world-famous Heracles

Led her as bride home to my house. Later, my son
Left his wife Megara and all her family here in Thebes,
Where I had settled, and set out for the Cyclopian
Fortress of Argos, eager to claim it as his home.
I had left Argos when I killed Electryon;
And so, to end my exile, and himself return
To the land of his fathers, Heracles undertook to cleanse
The earth of brutal violence. This was the high price
He offered Eurystheus for his own recall to Argos.
Whether Hera's jealousy, or Fate's decree, imposed
Such labours on him, who can say? He has accomplished
All but the last. Now through the jaws of Taenarus
He has gone down to Hades, to drag up to light
The triple-bodied hell-hound Cerberus; and we
Wait still for his return.

                    Now, many years ago,
So Theban legend says, before the sons of Zeus,
Those white-horsed charioteers Amphion and Zethus, ruled
This city of seven bastions, the throne was held
By one Lycus, husband of Dirce. His descendant,
Of the same name (a native of Euboea, not Thebes),
Finding our Theban citizens at each others' throats,
Attacked the town, killed Creon, and seized power him-
    self.
Now our alliance with the dead king has become
Our peril. With my son away, lost in the earth's depths,
This hero Lycus, now master of Thebes, resolves
To smother murder with more murder, and destroy
Heracles' sons, for fear they should grow up to avenge
Their murdered family. Megara too he means to kill;
And even me – an old feeble shadow of a man.

I was left here at home by my son Heracles
When he entered the black night of the lower world,

To guard his children. Now we all sit as suppliants
Of Zeus the Saviour at this altar, which was built
Once as a proud war-trophy by my noble son,
That day he overcame the Minyae. And here
We sit, without food, without drink; no other clothes;
The bare ground is our only bed; the palace doors
Are sealed against us. Help and hope are out of sight.
Some we thought friends have proved not so; while our true
    friends
Are powerless. Trouble is the surest test of friends.
The gods keep trouble far from any friend of mine.
MEGARA: Aged Amphitryon, who long ago led Thebes
To war against the Taphians, and destroyed their city,
How dark and devious are the ways of gods to men!
I was not born an outcast; Creon my father was
A byword for wealth, power, and fortune. He was a king,
Possessing that for lust of which long spears fly fast
Against the fortunate possessor. He had children;
And gave me as a royal bride to Heracles
Your son. Now all that life is flown, that splendour dead;
And you and I, and these three sons of Heracles,
Who nestle here like chicks under their mother's wing,
We all are at the point of death. These boys in turn
Keep questioning me. 'Mother,' they ask, 'where has he
    gone?
What is our father doing? When will he come back?'
They miss their father; they're too young to understand.
I put them off, tell them some tale to satisfy them.
Each time we hear the great gate open, up they jump,
Wondering if he has come, ready to run to him.

So now, father, what hope, what means to save our lives
Have you in mind? I look only to you. To escape
Over the frontier is impossible; there are guards
Posted on every road. We can no longer hope

For help from friends. Speak out, then: what is in your
    mind?

I fear we lose our time – and Death will not lose his.

AMPHITRYON: My daughter, it is no easy thing to give advice
    At times like this. Haste without care is little use.

MEGARA: Must things grow worse yet? Have you lost all love
    of life?

AMPHITRYON: Why, no. I love my life; and I still cling to
    hope.

MEGARA: I too; but we must not hope for the impossible.

AMPHITRYON: Remember, death deferred may always mean
    death foiled.

MEGARA: Oh, but the time of waiting is unbearable!

AMPHITRYON: Daughter, a fair wind may yet bring us safe
    to shore

From all our fears. My son, your husband, may yet come.
Be calm yourself, and dry your children's tear-filled eyes.
Your words must comfort them – your words, however sad,
Must lead their thoughts elsewhere. Misfortunes in the end
Grow tired of plaguing; storms in time blow themselves
    out.

So luck will change from man to man; and everything
Yields place to something else. Despair is cowardly;
The brave man holds fast to his confidence and hope.

Enter CHORUS *of Theban Elders.*

CHORUS:

I have come to the vaulted palace,
To the resting-place of this venerable king,
Leaning heavily on my staff;
My voice full of grief and mourning,
Like the sad chant of an aged swan;
A ghost of a man, voice with no substance,
Like a figure seen in a dream;
Even my voice quavers,
But it is the voice of a friend.

Children without a father, I weep for you;
For you too, Amphitryon, and you, unhappy mother
Mourning a husband lost in the lower world.

[*Addressing another Elder*] Come, put your best foot for-
    ward,
Like a horse that drags the weight of a wheeled wagon
Up some steep rocky path.
Any whose foothold is feeble or uncertain,
Grip the next man by the arm or the cloak.
Each of you help his fellow
Whom he fought beside long ago,
Spear level with spear,
When we were young together and went to battle,
And did not disgrace our glorious city.
            [*Several of the Chorus speak in turn.*]
— Look at this boy:
His eyes have the same fierce glare as his father's.

— Yes; their father's ill luck too
Has not deserted his sons.

— Nor his good looks either.

— O land of Hellas! If you lose these boys
You will be robbed of three noble champions.

Look, it is Lycus!
I see the king of Thebes, coming towards the palace.
            Enter LYCUS.
LYCUS: Now listen to me – you, Heracles' father, and you, his
    wife –
If I may question you; and, being your king, I may
Ask what I please: how long do you hope, by sitting here,
To lengthen out your life? What help do you expect?

Do you still trust that these boys' father will come back?

He's dead. [MEGARA *weeps*.] Why, are you not ashamed to
    wail and weep

Because you're going to die? – you, with your empty boast
Heard throughout Hellas, that you were co-partner with Zeus
In marriage and in parenthood; and you, again,
Styling yourself a hero's wife! What were they, then,
These marvellous exploits of your husband Heracles –
Destroying the swamp-serpent or the Nemean lion?
That lion he *said* he strangled with his hands; in fact
He snared it with a trap. Are such performances
Your weighty arguments for sparing his sons' lives?
Heracles won his fame by fighting animals;
In other matters he was no hero – he was nothing!
His left arm never held a shield; he never faced
An enemy's spear. He used a bow – the coward's weapon,
Handy for running away. The test of courage is not
Skill with a bow, but the firm foot, the unflinching eye
When the spear drives its hurtling furrow through the ranks.

My action now, Amphitryon, is not shamelessness,
But caution. I'm well aware I killed this woman's father
Creon; I hold his throne; so I've no wish to let
These boys grow up and live to take revenge on me.

AMPHITRYON: Let Zeus *act* in his son's behalf; I, Heracles,
Take it on me to *speak* for you, and show the depth
This man has sunk to. I'll not let his slander pass.

First, then, with gods as witnesses, I must rebut
His capital libel – yes, capital it is to call
You coward, Heracles. [*Turning to Lycus*] The thunderbolt
    of Zeus
Speaks of his deeds; and that swift chariot in which
He rode to war, planting winged arrows in the hearts
Of earth-born Giants, returning with the gods to sing

The victory-song. Or go to Pholoë, vile king,
And ask that savage tribe, the four-hoofed Centaurs, whom
They judge the bravest man on earth: whom but my son?
A sham, do you call him? What has Dirphys in Euboea,
Your native town, to say of *you*? Do people there
Call you a hero? In all Euboea there's not one place
Remembers you for one brave deed.

                              And then you sneer
At that superb discovery, the bow! Listen:
I'll teach you a little sense. A man with spear and shield
Is slave to his own arms. Suppose, to right or left,
The next man loses courage, he himself gets killed
Through others' cowardice; if he breaks his spear-shaft,
  how
Can he defend himself? He's lost his one resource.
While a skilled bowman has two great advantages:
First, he can shoot a thousand arrows, and still have more
To defend himself with; secondly, his fighting's done
Well out of reach – he wounds a watchful enemy
From perfect safety, with invisible stabs, and gives
No chance of striking back. In war it's common sense
To strike at every enemy within range, and keep
Your own skin whole. So in this argument my words
Contradict yours, and prove the exact opposite.

And then, these boys – why do you want to murder them?
What have they done? Perhaps it's reasonable that you,
A coward, should dread a hero's children. Yet it's hard
That we, as victims of your cowardice, must now
Be killed, instead of killing you – which would have been
Your fate, had Zeus dealt justly with the nobler side.
But, if you are resolved to keep the throne of Thebes,
Allow us to go forth as exiles. Shed no blood,
Lest yours be shed, when the wind turns in God's good time.

Oh, land of Cadmus! Yes, you too I turn to now
With words of bitterest reproach. Is this the help
You bring Heracles and his sons? – your champion, who
Alone battled with the whole tribe of Minyae,
And made Thebes face the world with free eyes once again?
Hellas too I accuse, and none shall silence me;
Hellas, whose duty was to march with fire and sword
To help these children, and repay their father's toil
Spent in the tireless purging of both sea and land.
But neither Thebes nor Hellas, children, takes your part.
You look at me: what am I but a ranting tongue?
I love you, but can't help you; all the strength I had
Is gone. I'm old; my limbs all shake; my fire is out.
If I were young and had the muscle I once had,
My sword would soon have bloodied his fair curling hair,
And he'd have fled in terror to the Atlantic coast!

CHORUS: A brave heart moves even a slow tongue to elo-
    quence.
LYCUS: Eloquence – yes! Talk on, pile words on words like
    towers.
I'll pay the malice of your words with deeds.
Here, men! Go, some to Parnassus, some to Helicon;
Get woodmen to cut logs of oak; bring them back here;
Heap them all round the altar and set fire to them;
Incinerate these five bodies! Let them understand
That *I* am king of Thebes now, not dead Heracles.

As for you Elders, who oppose my purposes –
You're weeping for these children? You'll have something
    else
To weep for, in good time: your houses laid in ruin.
Yes! Then you'll learn that I'm your king and you're my
    slaves.
CHORUS: Oh, earth-born Thebans! Are you not sons of
    dragon's teeth,

Which Ares ripped out of its ravenous jaw and sowed
In fertile earth? If so, stop leaning on those staves!
Up with them! Blood this murderer's head! He's no Cad-
    mean;
Shall true-born Thebans bow to a low foreigner?
– It won't pay you to come the tyrant over me;
And what I fought for never shall belong to you.
Get back to where you came from, play the braggart there!
While I have life and breath you shall not kill these boys.
Heracles left his children; but he has not plunged
So deep in earth that we forget him. You possess
His land, which you have ruined; he, who made it great,
Receives no fit reward. Am I a meddler, then,
To help a dead friend where he's most in need of help?
My right hand, how you long to grip a spear again!
But, being weak, you waste your wish. Had I been young
I would have made you swallow that word 'slave'; and we
Would have set up good government in Thebes, where you
Now take your pleasure. Faction and folly had driven
    Thebes
Insane, or she would never have got you for king.

MEGARA: I thank you. You are justly indignant, like true
    friends,
On our behalf. But do not, through your angry words,
Suffer yourselves. – Hear what I think, Amphitryon,
For what it's worth. I love my children – naturally;
I gave them birth, and care from childhood; and to me
Dying is fearful. Yet I count it foolishness
To struggle with the inevitable. Since we must die,
Let us not die shrivelled in fire, a mockery
To our enemies, which to me is a worse thing than death.
We owe a debt of honour to our royal house.
You were a famous fighter: it is unthinkable
That you should die a cowardly death. And I am wife
To one whose fair fame needs no witness to declare

That if these boys disgraced their name, he'd not lift hand
To save them. Noble hearts wince at their sons' dishonour;
I too have his example, and must follow it.

As for the hope you cherish, that your son will come
Back from the depths, I'll tell you what such hope is worth:
What dead man has returned to life from the dark world?
Or do you think words will make Lycus sorry for us?
Impossible! If your enemy is a man of honour
Or gentle birth, yield to him; you may touch his heart,
Perhaps win generous terms. If he's a rat – beware!

I thought just now, might we not beg, for these three boys,
Exile instead of death? But, to preserve their lives,
Then cumber them with poverty – a sordid fate!
It's truly said: exiles who call on friends for help
Soon learn that the warm welcoming smile will last one day.
Brave death with us; it's coming to you anyway.
Your blood, like ours, is royal; and we challenge you.
When the gods spread misfortune like a net, to try
To struggle out is folly more than bravery.
For what will be will be; no one can alter it.

CHORUS: Had anyone ill-treated you when my right arm
   Was stronger, he would soon have stopped. That time's long
      past;
   I'm finished. You yourself, Amphitryon, must find
   How best to break out from the closing trap of Fate.

AMPHITRYON: It's neither cowardice nor love of life that
      holds
   Me back from dying; only that I long to save
   These children for my son. But that's a useless wish;
   I cannot save them. [*He moves from the altar.*]

Here, then, my neck is ready for your sword. Strike home
With point or edge; or fling me from a rocky height.

One kindness, king, I beg you grant to me and her:
Kill us before the children, that we may not see
Them dying, hear them calling 'Mother! Grandfather!'
That would be intolerable. The rest – do as you please.
Nothing can help or save us.

MEGARA: I beseech you too,
Grant yet a second favour, both to him and me:
Unlock the palace doors, which now are closed to us;
Let me get funeral robes and put them on my sons,
To give them this small share of their inheritance.

LYCUS: You may do so. – Servants, unlock the doors. – Go in,
Dress yourselves; take what robes you please; and when
   you're dressed
I shall come back and send you to the world below.

            Exit LYCUS, *to one side of the stage.*

MEGARA: Children, come with me; come into your father's
   house.
Others possess his treasures; we still have his name.

        Exit MEGARA *with the children into the palace.*

AMPHITRYON: Zeus! I once thought you were my powerful
   friend. You shared
My marriage, shared my fatherhood of Heracles.
All this meant nothing; for you proved less powerful
Than you had seemed; and I, a man, put you, a god,
To shame. *I*'ve not betrayed the sons of Heracles.
You knew the way to steal into my bed, where none
Invited you, and lie with someone else's wife;
But those bound to you by every tie you cannot save.
This is strange ignorance in a god; or else, maybe,
Your very nature lacks a sense of right and wrong.

            Exit AMPHITRYON *to the palace.*

CHORUS:
Notes of joy blend with the tearful dirge
When Apollo's voice rings forth,
When with his golden plectrum

He rouses rich music from his lute.
I too will chant the praises
Of one who has entered the night of the world below
(Whether I am to name him Zeus-born,
Or the son of Amphitryon)
And honour his labours with a garland of song.
For the praise of their noble deeds
Is the glory of those departed.

First he purged the grove of Zeus
Of the lion that infested it;
And he wore on his back the lion's tawny skin,
And its fearful jaws framed his fair head.

Then with his deadly arrows
He struck the mountain breed of savage Centaurs,
And his wing'd shafts destroyed them.
Witness to his victory
Is the flashing water of Peneus,
The wide, level farmland where no crop grew,
The glens of Mount Pelion,
The shepherds' huts on the green slopes of Homole,
Where they plucked pine-trees for spears
And galloped ravaging over the plain of Thessaly.

Next, the dappled stag with golden horns
Which plundered a whole countryside,
Heracles killed, and dedicated
To the huntress goddess of Oenoë.

And he mounted Diomede's chariot
And with bit and bridle mastered the four wild stallions
That revelled in unnatural food
And gorged on human flesh,
Their jaws, their mangers, drenched in blood.

Pursuing his laboursome task for the king of Mycenae
He crossed the silver flow of Hebrus,
Followed the waters of Anaurus,
On to the sea-cliffs of Pelion, and there
Killed with his bow Cycnus the guest-murderer
Who lived in solitude near Amphanae.

Then to the distant West he travelled,
To the garden of the Singing Maidens,
To gather golden fruit from the leafy apple-tree,
And killed the dragon that coiled round it his flaming coils
To guard it from all comers.

He probed the inlets of the high seas
And made them safe for all men's ships.

He came to the mansion of Atlas,
And under the central arch of heaven stretched out his
    arms
And with his own strength upheld
The star-lit palaces of the gods.

Next he crossed the stormy Euxine Sea
To the land of the riding Amazons,
Where great rivers flow into Lake Maiotis,
Eager to win the gold-embroidered mantle
Of the warrior queen;
And from every part of Hellas
He gathered troops of followers,
Pursuing a girdle through blood and death.
And Hellas took the famous spoil of the Amazon,
Which now is preserved in Mycenae.

And the countless heads of that murderous hound,
The Lernean hydra, he severed and seared,

And smeared its gore on the arrows with which he killed
The herdsman of Erytheia, three-bodied Geryon.

As the crown of his journeys and glorious exploits
At last he took ship and set forth to Hades,
The world of tears, the end of labours;
There the doomed hero reaches the bound of life:
He has not returned.

His house is bare of friends;
Godless injustice sends his children
On the road whence none return,
And Charon's oar awaits them.
Your house, Heracles, looks to you for help,
And you are not here.

Oh! If I were young and strong
And could use a spear in a fight –
I and these friends of my youth –
We would have stood by your children
And saved them; but now
There is nothing left of the old splendid days.

Look, here they come, wearing robes of the dead –
The sons of Heracles, once called 'The Great',
And his wife leading her children by the hand,
And Heracles' father. What a sight!
Tears spring to my old eyes;
I cannot hold them back.

Enter AMPHITRYON, MEGARA, *and the* THREE BOYS.

MEGARA: Who acts as priest? Who wields the knife? The
    sacrifice
Stands ready for the road to death – a shameful, strange
Funeral procession; parents, children, old and young
Together, driven under one yoke. What bitter fate

Has doomed me and these children, whom I look on now
For the last time! – I gave you birth; but my fond care
Reared you for enemies to insult, rejoice over
And kill.

        How hope deceived me! – those bright hopes I drew
From words your father used to speak. You, eldest one,
Were to rule Argos, you were destined to possess
Eurystheus' palace and the rich Pelasgian plains;
He used to hang about your head the lion-skin cloak
Which was his own proud armour. You [*turning to the second
   child*] were king of Thebes
And all her chariots; these broad lands my father gave
To me, were your inheritance. You were his son:
You asked, he gave. Then he would place in your right
   hand,
Pretending it a gift, his huge carved fighting-club.
To you, his youngest, he would promise Oechalia,
The spoil, long since, of his far-conquering arrows. Thus,
Proudly and confidently, he planned for his three sons
Three firmly-founded thrones; while I would single out
For you the choicest brides, from Athens, Sparta, Thebes,
That such alliance, like stout stern-cables to a ship,
Might keep you safe and prosperous. This hope too is
   gone.
Fortune has turned, and for your brides has given you
The Maids of Death. My lustral water is all tears,
My joy all sorrow. See! Your father's father holds
Your wedding-feast, to seal this bitter bond with Death.

Oh, children! let me clasp you close – who shall be first?
Who last? Come, let me kiss you, cling to you. You weep,
My pretty flowers! Then, like a brown-winged honey-bee,
From all your weeping I'll distil one precious tear,
And shed it for you.

Dear husband! If a word spoken on earth can reach
The ears of those below, I call you, Heracles!
Your father and your sons are near to death; I too,
Your wife, whom all called fortunate, am perishing!
Come! Help us! Even as a ghost, appear to me –
No more is needed! Only come, and we are saved!

AMPHITRYON: You make your prayer, my daughter, to the
    powers below;
I'll stretch my hands to Heaven. O Zeus, I call on you:
If you will help these children, save them now, come now.
Soon it will be too late. – Oh, I've prayed many times;
I waste my breath. We can't escape now; we must die.
[*To the Chorus*] Friends, life's a brief and trivial thing. Such
    as it is,
As you pass through, find as much pleasure as you can,
From dawn till nightfall keeping sorrow at arm's length.
Time as he flies has no care to preserve our hopes;
He's bent on his own business. Look at me: I once
Was great in action, drew all eyes upon me; now
In one day Fortune has snatched from me everything,
As the wind blows a feather to the sky; all lost.
Wealth, reputation – who holds them with certainty?
I know none. Farewell. Since we all were young, you've
    been
My friends: this is the last time you will see me here.

MEGARA: Oh, look, look!
Who is it? Can it be my husband, Heracles?

AMPHITRYON: I don't know, daughter. I am speechless.

MEGARA: We were told
That he was dead. Can this be he?

AMPHITRYON: It's Heracles –
Unless we're dreaming in broad daylight.

MEGARA: It's no dream!
Does grief create such visions? It is Heracles!
It is your son, and no one else. – Come, children, run,

Cling to your father's robe, and never let him go.
He is no less a saviour to you than Zeus himself.

Enter HERACLES.

HERACLES: Greeting, my house! And greeting, doorway to
   my hearth!
   What happiness to see you, as I come at last
   Back to the living world! – Why, what is this? My sons
   In funeral dress, wreaths of the dying on their heads!
   A crowd of men – and there, my wife! My father too!
   All weeping! What has happened? I must question them.
   Megara, my wife! What is it? What has happened here?

MEGARA: O dearest husband!

AMPHITRYON: Dear son, light of my old eyes!

MEGARA: You're safe! You've come – to save our lives at the
   last moment.

HERACLES: Your lives? What is this, father? Have you trouble
   here?

MEGARA: They are killing us! – Forgive me, Sir, if I speak
   first,
   Which is your right. Women are readier than men
   To tell their grief. – My sons were dying; so was I.

HERACLES: By great Apollo! What will you tell me next?

MEGARA: My brothers
   Are dead, my father too.

HERACLES: But how? Who struck them down?

MEGARA: Lycus murdered them – he is the new king of
   Thebes.

HERACLES: Did he make war on the city? Or was there civil
   war?

MEGARA: Thebes was divided. He now holds the seven gates.

HERACLES: And what was threatened against you and Amphitryon?

MEGARA: He meant to kill your father and your sons and me.

HERACLES: Kill you? How could my fatherless sons put him
   in fear?

MEGARA: He feared they might one day avenge my father's
 death.

HERACLES: But why are you all dressed like this, in burial
 robes?

MEGARA: We put them on just now, to be prepared for death.

HERACLES: And he was going to kill you – you, my family?

MEGARA: We had no friends to help us; you, we heard, were
 dead.

HERACLES: What made you give up hope of me?

MEGARA: Eurystheus kept
 Sending reports –

HERACLES: I see. Why did you leave my house?

MEGARA: They turned us out. Your father was flung from his
 bed.

HERACLES: He'd ill-treat an old man? Has he no decency?

MEGARA: Decency's a divinity he doesn't know.

HERACLES: But – in my absence, what became of all our
 friends?

MEGARA: When a man meets misfortune, who stays true to
 him?

HERACLES: They shrugged off all I went through in the
 Minyan war?

MEGARA: Of course. Luckless is friendless, as I said just now.

HERACLES: Come, throw away these funeral wreaths! Lift
 up your eyes!

Look! You have light for darkness, life instead of death.
Now I must go; my hand has work to do. And first
To level with the ground the house of this new king,
Cut off his head, and throw it out for dogs to tear;
Then, for the citizens of Cadmus – those I find
Have paid my benefits with treachery, this club,
Veteran of many victories, shall deal with them;
Or with my feathered barbs I'll scatter them, and fill
Ismenus full of corpses, make the limpid stream
Of Dirce run red. Should I not help my wife, my sons,

My father, before the rest of the world? Good-bye to all
My famous labours! They're a waste of time, while I
Neglect to help my own. These boys were to be killed
For bearing my name; then in their defence I must
Die, if need be. At Eurystheus' command I fought
The hydra and the lion: what honour comes of that
Unless I avenge the threat to my own children's lives?
I'd never again be known as Conquering Heracles.

CHORUS: They are your sons: it is right to take revenge for
them,
And no less for your aged father and your wife.

AMPHITRYON: It is like you, my noble son, to love your
friends
And hate your enemies. Yet, don't act too hastily.

HERACLES: Does something of what I propose seem rash to
you?

AMPHITRYON: There's a large class of needy men, who make
a show
Of being prosperous; Lycus has their strong support.
They raised the riots; they sold Thebes to slavery
In hope of lawless plunder, to redeem their own
Bankruptcy, caused by extravagance and idleness.
You were seen entering Thebes. The news of your return
Will bring your enemies flocking; so be on your guard.

HERACLES: If the whole city saw me, what do I care? How-
ever,
An omen warned me – a bird in the wrong quarter; so,
Foreseeing trouble, I came here by a secret path.

AMPHITRYON: Good. Go in now; salute the gods of the
hearth, and show
Your face to your own home. The king will come himself
To drag your wife, your sons, and me away to slaughter.
Stay in the house, and all will fall into your hands;
You'll win in safety. Don't excite your citizens,
My son, till you've made all secure here in the house.

HERACLES: That's good advice; I'll follow it, and go indoors.
Now I've returned at last out of the sunless caves
Of Hades and Persephone, I will not neglect
To pay first honours to the gods who keep our home.

AMPHITRYON: My son, did you in truth enter the world of
death?

HERACLES: Yes, and dragged up to earth three-headed Cerberus.

AMPHITRYON: You fought and forced him? Or was he
Persephone's gift?

HERACLES: I fought him. I had beheld the holy Mysteries;
That gave me strength.

AMPHITRYON: Who keeps him now? Eurystheus?
HERACLES: No;
He's at Hermione, in Demeter's sacred grove.

AMPHITRYON: And does Eurystheus know that you've
returned to earth?

HERACLES: No; I resolved to learn first how the land lay
here.

AMPHITRYON: Why did you stay so long below the earth?
HERACLES: Theseus
Was there, held prisoner; I delayed to rescue him.

AMPHITRYON: And where is he? Has he gone home?
HERACLES: To Athens – yes,
Joyful at his escape. – But come with me, my boys,
Into your father's house. You're happier going in
Than you were coming out! Cheer up now; no more tears.
And you, my wife, stop trembling, and compose yourself.
Children, stop clinging to my cloak! I'll not take wing
Or try to run away from you! – Why, look at this!
They hold on all the tighter, they will not let go.
Were you so near to death? Come, then, and hold my
hands;
I'll take these little ships in tow. I never find
Children a trouble. All men are the same at heart

Towards children. Some are of high birth, some of low; some rich,
Some poor; but all love children – every human soul.

They all go into the palace.

CHORUS:

Youth is what I love.
Age weighs on my head like a burden
Heavier than the rocks of Etna;
It draws a curtain of darkness before my eyes.
Not the wealth of an Eastern throne,
Not a palace full of gold
Would I take in exchange for youth.
Youth is most precious in prosperity,
Most precious in poverty;
Age is miserable, tainted with death:
I hate it. Away with it, let the sea swallow it!
Why must the curse of age fall on men's homes and cities?
Away to the winds with it!

If the gods had understanding
And wisdom, as men conceive it,
A second youth should be awarded
To distinguish those whose lives were virtuous.
Such men after one death
Would rise again into the sun's beams
And run a double course of life,
While ignoble natures enjoyed but one span.
In this way it would be possible
To distinguish good men from bad,
As through the rifts of murky clouds
A sailor sees the bright company of stars.
But gods make no clear division
Between goodness and wickedness;
Time, as the years turn,
Brings no more than increase of wealth.

I will never grow tired
Of joining Victory, gift of the Graces,
In perfect marriage with music and song.
Where songs are not heard, there is no life for me;
Let me live amidst the crowning of poets.
Even an aged singer
Still has memory, and sings her praises;
I can still chant the victory-song of Heracles,
Either where Bacchus pours his gift of wine,
Or where music flows
From seven-stringed lyre and Libyan pipe.
I am not yet too old to serve the Muses,
Who taught me their secrets.

Triumph-songs are sung by girls of Delos
As they turn in the graceful dance by the temple doors
Of Leto's glorious son;
And I will sing a triumph here at your door,
Raising my swan-song from grey-bearded lips.
I have a splendid theme: Heracles
Is the son of Zeus;
And has surpassed the glory of his birth
With the labours of his noble life;
By destroying beasts of which men lived in terror
He won for us the tranquillity we enjoy.

Enter LYCUS, *attended, from the side of the stage, and* AMPHI-
TRYON *from the palace.*

LYCUS: Amphitryon, you're none too soon in coming out.
You've been a long time, all of you, dressing yourselves
In funeral vestments. Go on, call his wife and sons,
Tell them to show themselves out here; those were our
terms –
On your part voluntary; you agreed to die.

AMPHITRYON: King, you grind down my wretchedness. My
son is dead:

You taunt me with that loss. You should, strong as you are,
Observe some measure in your eagerness. You say
That we must die. So be it, then; perform your will.

LYCUS: Well, where is Megara? Where are Heracles' three
    sons?

AMPHITRYON [*looking at the palace door*]: So far as I can tell
    from here, I think –

LYCUS: You think?
    What do you think?

AMPHITRYON: – She is sitting as a suppliant
    On the altar-steps.

LYCUS: Well, sitting there won't save her life.

AMPHITRYON: She's calling hopelessly on her dead husband's
    name.

LYCUS: He'll never come back.

AMPHITRYON: No; unless indeed some god
    Should raise him from the dead.

LYCUS: Go in and fetch her out.

AMPHITRYON: If I did, then I would be part-guilty of her
    blood.

LYCUS: All right. Since you have scruples – I have none, nor
    fears.
    I'll go myself and fetch them all. Men, follow me.
    She's playing for time – I'll gladly deal with this delay.

                Exit LYCUS *with attendants.*

AMPHITRYON: Go, then; a fitting end awaits you. Someone
    else,
    Perhaps, will see to what remains. Your acts were harsh;
    Expect a harsh fate. – Friends, his going is well timed.
    He'll slip into the snare; the evil-hearted coward,
    Planning to kill, will meet the sword's point. I will go
    And see him fall dead. What joy, when an enemy
    Pays with his blood the just price of his wicked deeds.

CHORUS:
    Cruelty and suffering have changed sides;

The life of a once powerful king
Flows back to the gulf of death.
Hail the justice of Heaven, the equity of Fate!
Now at last you stand where your blood shall pay your
    debt
For insolent oppression of your betters.
Tears of joy start from my eyes.
A fate he would never have thought possible
Has recoiled upon King Lycus.
Come, friend, let us look inside the house,
To see if all goes as we would wish.

    A shriek is heard from inside the palace.

CHORUS:

 Listen – the opening note of a song I long to hear!
 Death is close; and the king
 Knows, and greets it with a groan of terror.

LYCUS [*within*]: O land of Cadmus, I am treacherously mur-
    dered!

CHORUS:

 You were a murderer; for all your wickedness
 This is just revenge; you must endure it.

 Who was the man of mortal flesh
 Who, uttering lawless blasphemy,
 Challenged with foolish words the gods of heaven,
 And said they have no power?

 Friends, that wicked man is dead.
 The house is silent. Come, dance for joy;
 Our hopes are answered; those we love have won.
 The music of dance and feast
 Rings through the holy city of Thebes.
 Fortune has turned – tears are forgotten;
 Fortune has turned – troubles are ended,
 Songs of joy are born.

The usurper has gone;
Our former king rules again,
Safe home from the harbour of death;
Hope beyond all hopes has come to us.

The gods, the gods take heed of men;
They observe wickedness and goodness.
Gold, with good fortune,
Yoked to the chariot of mortal life,
Speeds it along the course of pride;
On their flank is harnessed unscrupulous power.
The reckless driver gives never a glance
At the return course, the time yet to come.
He hurtles ahead of Law,
Gives rein to his lawless will,
Smashes his own success in full career,
And the dark dust covers him.

Put on garlands, River Ismenus!
Trim streets of seven-gated Thebes,
Bright waters of Dirce,
Break into dancing!
You too, nymphs of Asopus,
Come from your parent stream,
Join us in singing of Heracles,
His fight and his glorious victory!
O wooded crag of Delphi,
O haunts of the Muses of Helicon,
Let your shouts of rejoicing ring every echo
Through the walls and ways of my city!
The city where the Sown Men sprang up,
An army with brazen shields, whose children's chil-
    dren,
Rising for Thebes like the holy dawn,
Inherit this land in continual succession.

177

O bed where two begetters lay in love,
One a mortal; the other Zeus,
Who came to embrace Alcmene daughter of Perseus!
It is many years now
Since I abandoned my early doubts,
And believed that you, divine Zeus, lay with her;
For the passing of time has made shine in the eyes of the
    world
The greatness of Heracles,
Who came out from the palace of Pluto,
Up from the deep chambers of earth.

I judge you, Heracles, more fit by birth to rule
Than the mean king of yesterday.
He, when made to hold a sword and fight,
Provides a plain answer to all men's question –
Whether the gods still favour a just cause.

      IRIS *and* MADNESS *appear above the palace roof.*

CHORUS:
    Look there, look there!
    Are you as terrified as I
    At the horrible figures standing over the palace?
    Escape, escape! Don't stand staring,
    Move quickly, get away from them.
    Apollo, Saviour! Deliver us from evil!

IRIS: Elders, take heart! You need not tremble at this vision.
  You see here Madness, daughter of Night, and me, Iris,
  Servant of the gods. We bring no harm to Thebes, but aim
  Our stroke at one man's house, whom Zeus begot, they say,
  Of Alcmene. Before he had accomplished all
  His fearful labours, Fate preserved him, nor would Zeus
  His father permit me or Hera to raise hand
  Against him; but, now that he has performed in full
  Eurystheus' tasks, Hera desires (and I am with her)
  To fasten on Heracles the guilt of kindred blood,

Making him kill his children. Come, then, virgin child
Of murky Night, close up your heart against all pity,
Send maniac fury on this man, distort his mind
With lust for his own children's blood, cut murder's cable,
Rack him with lunatic convulsions; that when he
With guilt-red hand has sent his crown of lovely sons
Over the river of death, he may perceive how hot
Is Hera's anger against him, and learn my hate too.
If Heracles escape our punishment, then gods
Are nowhere, and the mortal race may rule the earth.

MADNESS: My nature's noble, as my parents were – Heaven
My father, Night my mother; and my privilege
Is not to take delight in slaughter, nor do I
With pleasure visit cities. So I wish to plead
With Hera and you, before I see her fall into
Unwisdom; hoping you may listen. Heracles,
Whose house you now send me to ravage, is a man
Famous alike on earth and among gods. He tamed
Untrodden lands, seas full of monsters; he alone
Restored the worship due to gods, fallen to decay
Through men's impiety.

IRIS: This plan is Hera's wish
And mine; so spare us your advice.

MADNESS: I only thought
How I might turn your path towards good instead of evil.

IRIS: The Queen of Heaven did not send you here to think.

MADNESS: The sun's my witness that I act against my will.
But if I must indeed perform Hera's resolve –
And yours – at once, and follow in full cry, as hounds
Follow the hunt, I'll go; and not the groaning sea's
Violence, not earthquakes, nor the gasping agonies
Of thunderbolts, shall match my fury as I strike
Heracles to the heart, shatter his house, rage through
His rooms, killing his children first; he who is doomed
To be their murderer shall not know they are the sons

Of his own body, till my frenzy leaves him. Look!
See him – head wildly tossing – at the starting-point,
Silent, his rolling eyeballs full of maniac fire;
Breathing convulsively, and with a terrible
Deep bellow, like a bull about to charge, he shrieks
To all Hell's fiends – I'll plague you worse yet! You shall
    dance
In terror to my piping! – Iris, wing your way
Back to Olympus. I'll enter this house unseen.

> *Exit* IRIS, *above;* MADNESS *enters the palace.*

CHORUS:

> O city of Thebes, weep and lament!
> Your choice flower is cut down.
> Unhappy Hellas, you will lose
> The son of Zeus, your benefactor;
> You will lose him, rapt and frenzied
> By the tuneless music of Madness.
>
> Madness has mounted her chariot;
> Groans and tears accompany her.
> She plies the lash, hell-bent for murder,
> Rage gleaming from her eyes,
> A Gorgon of Night, and around her
> Bristle the hissing heads of a hundred snakes.
>
> Swiftly doom has undone success;
> Swiftly his sons shall die by their father's hand.
> Oh, pity, pity! Zeus, do you hear?
> Fiends of jealousy, mad for revenge,
> Will fall like tearing wolves on your unhappy son!
>
> Listen, walls and roofs of the palace!
> Do you hear a rhythmic beat beginning?
> Not for the dance of Cybele's cymbals,
> Not with the joy of the Bacchic thyrsus,

Or the dark outpouring of the ripe grape;
But for blood.

Run, children, escape!
This maddening music is deadly –
A hunting-horn of death!
– Listen: he is after them, hunts them down.
Can Madness riot through the house
And not fulfil her purpose?
Oh, what misery, what suffering!
How I weep for his father, and for Megara
Who bore and reared his sons for this!

Look! Look now! A whirlwind shakes the house,
The roof is shattered. – Stop! Stop!
What are you doing, son of Zeus?
Destroying your palace with a hurricane of hell,
As Athene destroyed Enceladus?

Enter from the palace a MESSENGER, *weeping*.

MESSENGER: Oh, sirs! Oh, sirs!

CHORUS: What is it? What are you crying for?

MESSENGER: What has happened in there – it is unspeakable!

CHORUS: Indeed I believe you.

MESSENGER: The children are dead.

CHORUS: Oh! How horrible!

MESSENGER: It is indeed horrible.

CHORUS: How cruel to kill them! How could a father be so savage?

MESSENGER: What we have suffered is more than words can tell.

CHORUS: A fate, a pitiful fate their father brought on them.
How will you describe it? Speak, tell us what happened
When this heaven-sent disaster struck the house;
How did the children die?

MESSENGER: There by the altar stood victims for sacrifice
　　To cleanse the house; for Heracles had killed the king
　　And thrown his body out of doors. And the three boys –
　　A lovely group they made – were there with Megara
　　And old Amphitryon; and the knife and barley-meal
　　Had now circled the altar. No one spoke a word.
　　Heracles was about to lift the lighted torch
　　And dip it in the holy water; there he stood
　　Silent, and hesitating. His sons looked at him.
　　His face had changed; his eyeballs rolled unnaturally,
　　Showing their roots all bloodshot; down his curling beard
　　A white froth trickled. Then with a maniac laugh he cried,
　　'Why am I offering sacrifice and cleansing fire
　　Now, father – when I'll have it all to do again?
　　I haven't killed Eurystheus yet! I'm going to fetch
　　Eurystheus' head here; then in a single ceremony
　　I'll wash my hands of *him* and those I killed today.
　　Fling out that water, throw those baskets down! My bow –
　　Bring it me, someone! Bring my club! I'm setting out
　　Against Mycenae. Bring crowbars and pickaxes;
　　We'll lever up their strong Cyclopian masonry
　　Fitted with line and hammer – iron will prize it open.'
　　Then he pretended he had a chariot; leapt in,
　　Gripped on the rail, and, like a man using a goad,
　　Kept thrusting. All his servants looked at one another,
　　Laughing, yet terrified, saying, 'Is this a joke
　　Our master's playing on us, or is he raving mad?'
　　Then, running to and fro about the house, he burst
　　Into the men's hall, said he'd arrived at Megara –
　　Right there in his own house! He sat down on the floor,
　　Just as he was, and started to prepare a meal.
　　He stayed at that only a moment, then cried out,
　　'I'm near the woods of Corinth now!' Then he unpinned
　　His cloak, stood naked, and began a wrestling-match
　　With no one; then proclaimed to an invisible crowd

Himself as victor. Then he was at Mycenae, loud
In threats against Eurystheus. But Amphitryon
Clung to his mighty hand, and cried, 'O dearest son,
What is this madness? Surely killing Lycus here
Has not deranged you?' Heracles imagined this
Was the father of Eurystheus clinging to his hand,
Trembling with fear. He pushed him back; handled his bow
And quiver, ready to shoot his own sons, thinking they
Were children of Eurystheus. Terrified, they rushed
This way and that; one hid behind his mother's dress,
One in the shadow of a pillar, one behind
The altar cowered like a bird. Megara shrieked,
'What are you doing? They're your children!' Amphitryon
And all the servants shrieked. Nimbly and swiftly he
Spun round the pillar, faced the child, and shot him dead.
He fell back gasping, spattering the stone with blood.
Heracles yelled in triumph; 'There lies one,' he cried,
'One of Eurystheus' cubs has paid his father's debt.'
Down by the altar steps, hoping he was unseen,
Another boy was crouching. Heracles aimed at him;
The child was quicker – he darted to his father's knees,
Reached for his beard and neck, and cried, 'I am your son –
Yours, not Eurystheus'. Father dear, don't kill your son!'
His father's eyes were like a Gorgon's – twisted, cruel.
He could not use his arrows – the boy stood too close;
So, like a blacksmith forging iron, he raised his club
High, and upon his son's fair head he crashed it down,
Shattering the skull. His second victim dead, he now
Made for the third; but Megara swiftly snatched the child
Away, and rushed with him into an inner room
And locked the doors. He, just as if this were in truth
Mycenae and the Cyclopian walls, with pick and bar
Heaved, hammered, burst the door-posts, and with a single
    shot
Dispatched both wife and child. Then he went charging back

To kill his father. But a phantom came – it seemed
To us like Pallas, with plumed helmet, brandishing
A spear, and hurled a boulder full against his chest,
Which checked his murderous fury, stunned him, and he
    fell
Senseless to the ground, striking his back against a pillar
Which, broken in two by the collapsing roof, lay propped
Against its base. We who had taken flight came back
And helped Amphitryon tie him fast with harness-cords
To the pillar, so that when sleep left him he might not
Add crime to crime. He's sleeping now. Sleep is a blessing –
But not to one who has killed his wife and his three sons.
Indeed, I know of no man more unblest than he.

Exit MESSENGER.

CHORUS: The slaughter done in Argos by the daughters of
    Danaus
Was in its day the most famous in Hellas;
But today's bloodshed surpasses it,
Leaves far behind what happened then.
I may cite the tale, hallowed by poetic use,
Of Procne, who killed her royal son;
But he was an only child; while you, Heracles,
Were doomed to destroy in one demented moment
Three sons of your own begetting.
How can I find tears for grief so bitter?
What funeral song, what mourning ritual will suffice?

[*The palace doors open, and reveal the bodies of* MEGARA *and
    the children, with* AMPHITRYON *mourning over them; and*
                    HERACLES *bound to a pillar.*]

Look! The lofty doors of the palace
Are moving, parting, opening.
Oh! What a pitiful sight –
These children lying before their unhappy father!
After child-murder he sleeps – a dreadful sleep.
Fetters and knotted cords

Wound around his resting body
Bind him fast to the stone pillar.
And here is his aged father –
A bitter path he has to tread! –
Mourning as a bird mourns for her unfledged young.

AMPHITRYON:

Elders of Thebes, be quiet, quiet!
While he is relaxed in sleep
Let him forget his sufferings.

CHORUS:

My tears flow for you, Amphitryon,
And for these children,
And for the hero of many victories.

AMPHITRYON:

Stand farther off; no sound, no voice!
He is sleeping calmly, do not break his rest.

CHORUS:

How terrible a deed!

AMPHITRYON:

No, no! You kill me.

CHORUS:

The blood he shed rises to accuse him.

AMPHITRYON:

Friends, will you not lament more softly?
I fear he will wake, tear off his fetters,
Run murdering through the city,
Kill his father and destroy his house.

CHORUS:

I must weep; I cannot help it.

AMPHITRYON:

Hush! I will go close and listen to his breathing.

CHORUS:

Is he asleep?

AMPHITRYON:

Yes. Oh, what a sleep! An accursed sleep.

Wife-murderer! Child-murderer!
Master of the bow-string's deadly music!

CHORUS:

Weep for them.

AMPHITRYON:

I weep.

CHORUS:

For the children's death.

AMPHITRYON:

Oh, cruel!

CHORUS:

For your son Heracles.

AMPHITRYON:

My son!

CHORUS:

Amphitryon –

AMPHITRYON [*bending over Heracles*]:

Be quiet now, quiet!
He is turning, twisting; he is waking.
I must go indoors and hide!

CHORUS: You need not be afraid; it is still night with him.

AMPHITRYON:

Look – look at him.
It is not dying that I fear
After the pain of my unhappy life;
But I fear he may kill his father,
Add evil to evil, and beside his present guilt
Bear the stain of a parent's blood.

CHORUS:

Had you but died in your hour of youth and glory,
When for your wife's sake you went forth
To avenge the blood of her brothers,
And destroyed the Taphians and their town!

AMPHITRYON:

Quickly, friends, escape; he is waking;

Away from the house, away from the madman!
Soon he'll be raging through the city
Heaping murder on murder.

CHORUS: O Zeus, why had you this fierce hate against your
son?

Why must he pass through such a sea of suffering?

With a loud cry HERACLES *wakes.*

HERACLES: I am alive, I breathe; I see all I should see,
The sky, the earth, the sun's bright archery; and yet
My mind feels drowned in waves of turmoil, and my breath
Comes hot, unsteady, not calm as it should. – What's this?
Moored like a ship! Ropes round my chest – me, Heracles!
– My arms lashed to this piece of broken masonry;
Sitting – and corpses here beside me! Feathered arrows
Scattered about; – my bow! which often stood by me
In battle, and guarded me as I have treasured it.
Did I descend a second time to the dead world,
Having once for Eurystheus traced that double course?
I see no sign of Sisyphus and his rolling rock,
Or Pluto, or the sceptre of Persephone.
I feel stunned. Why am I lying helpless? Where am I?
Hullo! Is any friend of mine here, anywhere,
To tell me where I am, what has been happening?
I understand nothing that I should understand.

AMPHITRYON: My son, my sorrow! – Old friends, shall I go
to him?

CHORUS: Yes; I'll go with you, and help you bear this bitterness.

HERACLES: Dear father, why do you weep? Why do you veil
your eyes,
Standing so far away from me? I am your son.

AMPHITRYON: My son! Yes, even abased and stricken, still
my son!

HERACLES: Stricken? How stricken, father? Why this flood
of tears?

187

AMPHITRYON: What you have suffered would bring groans
even from a god.

HERACLES: So terrible? What is it? You have not told me
yet.

AMPHITRYON: You see yourself, if now your mind is sound
again.

HERACLES: You hint at some disaster for me. Is it so?

AMPHITRYON: If you're no more a frenzied celebrant of
Death,
I'll tell you.

HERACLES: Still these mysteries! I guess and fear.

AMPHITRYON: I am still doubtful if your mind is well
restored.

HERACLES: My mind was frenzied? How? I don't remember
it.

AMPHITRYON: Old friends, shall I unbind him? What ought
I to do?

HERACLES: Unbind me; and say who bound me – he's my
enemy.

AMPHITRYON: Let what you know and see suffice you; ask
no more.

HERACLES: I tell you, silence is no answer: I must know.

AMPHITRYON [unbinding him]: Zeus, do you see that Hera on
her throne is cause
Of all this misery?

HERACLES: Hera! Has *she* struck at me?

AMPHITRYON: Forget her; be concerned with your own
ruined life.

HERACLES: Ruined? You are going to tell me of some
calamity?

AMPHITRYON: Look at these children's bodies, lying where
they fell.

HERACLES: Oh, gods! What do I see?

AMPHITRYON: They were no enemies,
These children you took arms against, my son.

HERACLES: Took arms?
What do you mean? Who killed them?

AMPHITRYON: You, son, and your bow,
And whatsoever god it was that drove you to it.

HERACLES: What did I do? Father, what horror you reveal!

AMPHITRYON: You were stark mad – To tell you this is
agony.

HERACLES: My wife too? Did I kill her too?

AMPHITRYON: All is the work
Of your sole hand.

HERACLES: Oh! Pain swallows me like a cloud.

AMPHITRYON: My tears are for your pain, my pity for their
death.

HERACLES: Did I tear down my own house, or drive others
on?

AMPHITRYON: I know only one thing: your whole life is in
ruin.

HERACLES: But where did this disastrous frenzy come on
me?

AMPHITRYON: By the altar, as you cleansed your hands with
sacrifice.

HERACLES: What shame, what misery! To become the
murderer
Of my most dear sons! Why do I not take my life?
Leap from some bare cliff, aim a sword at my own heart,
Become myself the avenger of my children's blood?
Or burn my flesh with fire, to avert the infamy
Which now awaits me?

                    [THESEUS *is seen approaching.*]
                          But see! To prevent these thoughts
Of death, here Theseus comes, my kinsman and my friend.
I shall be seen; and the pollution of my deeds
Defile his sight, who is the dearest of my friends.
What shall I do? Where can I find a solitude
For wretchedness, in height or depth? I must conceal

189

My head from daylight. I am ashamed of my deep guilt.
I have no wish to harm the innocent, to cast
The curse of unrequited blood on a friend's head.

HERACLES wraps his head in his cloak.
Enter THESEUS, attended.

THESEUS: I have come, Amphitryon, with an Athenian armed
    force,
Who are waiting down at the riverside, to bring your son
My help in war. There came to Athens a report
That Lycus with an army had invaded Thebes
And seized the throne. So, old friend, if you stand in need
Of allies, or of my hand's service, here I am,
Ready to pay the debt I owe to Heracles
For rescue from the lower world. – But what is this?
A field of dead! Have I come on the heels of crime?
Am I too late? Who killed these children? And whose
    wife
Is this? Young children don't stand fighting in the ranks!
Surely what I see here's not war, but wickedness.

AMPHITRYON: O king of the olive-crowned hill of Athens! –

THESEUS: Your first words sound like a cry of sorrow.

AMPHITRYON: We have been grievously struck by the hand
    of Heaven.

THESEUS: Who are these children you are weeping over?

AMPHITRYON: My poor son was their father, and he killed
    them;
    Their father, and he is defiled with the guilt of their blood.

THESEUS: Tell me something less horrible.

AMPHITRYON: If only I could!

THESEUS: What a fearful thing!

AMPHITRYON: Our whole life is vanished with the wind.

THESEUS: What did he do? Tell me.

AMPHITRYON:
    He was adrift in a storm of insanity;
    And his arrows were dipped in the hydra's blood.

THESEUS:

    Hera's hand was in this.

    But who is that, sitting beside the bodies?

AMPHITRYON:

    That is my son, Heracles of many labours,

    Who carried his shield beside the gods

    In battle with murderous Giants on the Phlegraean plain.

THESEUS:

    Has any man ever suffered as he has?

AMPHITRYON:

    You could find no man his equal

    For endless travel or for brave endurance.

THESEUS:

    Why does he cover his head in his cloak?

AMPHITRYON:

    He is ashamed in your presence;

    Ashamed before the love of his own kin,

    And the blood of his children.

THESEUS:

    But I am here to share his grief. Unveil his head.

AMPHITRYON:

    My son, take your cloak from your face;

    Throw it off, show yourself to the sun.

    [*To Theseus*] His weight of sorrow dries up all his tears.

    – My son, I beg you, by your beard, your knees,

    Your hand, while the tears flow from my old eyes!

    Restrain your desperate, lionlike mood, dear son;

    Distress drives you to think of death;

    But such a course would defy the gods,

    And only add wrong to wrong.

THESEUS: You who sit there in utter misery, look up

  And show your friend your face. There is no darkness bears

  A cloak so black as could conceal your suffering.

  Why wave your hand to warn me of the taint of blood?

  For fear your words pollute me? I am not afraid

To share your deep affliction with you, as I shared
Your victory. This bond was made between us when
You brought me back from darkness to the world of light.
I hate a friend whose gratitude grows dim with age;
One who'll enjoy his friend's prosperity, but not
Sail with him in rough weather. Come, unwrap your head;
Stand up; look at me, Heracles. A noble heart
Endures the strokes of gods or Fate, and does not flinch.

THESEUS *uncovers Heracles' head.*

HERACLES: Have you seen, Theseus, what I did to my three
sons?

THESEUS: They told me, and I see.

HERACLES: Why then have you uncovered
My head before the sun?

THESEUS: A god is not defiled
By what is mortal.

HERACLES: I am unclean. Keep far away!

THESEUS: No curse infects from friend to friend.

HERACLES: You must not be
My friend; yet I cannot regret that I was yours.

THESEUS: You gave me help then; now I give you sympathy.

HERACLES: Can you have sympathy for me who killed my sons?

THESEUS: Yes; now that things have changed with you – I
weep for you.

HERACLES: Have you known any man more utterly struck
down?

THESEUS: Your sorrows reach from earth to heaven.

HERACLES: That is why
I am resolved to end my life.

THESEUS: You think the gods
Care for your threats?

HERACLES: Divinity's impervious
To human feeling. I defy divinity.

THESEUS: Restrain your speech. Proud words may bring more
suffering.

192

HERACLES: I am brim-full of suffering, there's no room for
   more.

THESEUS: What will you do? Where will defiance lead you
   now?

HERACLES: To death; back to the nether world I have just
   left.

THESEUS: You speak now like some common, ordinary man.

HERACLES: And you, untouched by sorrow, give *me* good
   advice!

THESEUS: Is it the all-enduring Heracles who speaks?

HERACLES: Never such pain as this. Endurance must have
   bounds.

THESEUS: – Heracles, mankind's greatest friend and benefactor?

HERACLES: Mankind – what help are they? Power is in
   Hera's hand.

THESEUS: For *you* – a fool's death? Hellas would not stomach
   it!

HERACLES: Listen then: here are reasons to oppose the
   advice
   You give me. I'll explain to you that my whole life,
   Both past and present, ought not to have been at all.
   First, then: I am my father's son. When Amphitryon
   Married my mother Alcmene, he was guilty of
   Her father's blood, and so accursed. When a family
   Stands on unsound foundations, no prosperity
   Follows its sons. Then, Zeus – whoever Zeus may be –
   Begot me as the mark for Hera's enmity.
   – Do not be vexed, Amphitryon; it is you I count
   My father, not Zeus. – Then, when I was a mere babe
   Still at the breast, the Queen of Heaven placed fierce-eyed
      snakes
   Inside my cradle to destroy me. When I grew up
   And strong flesh wrapped my limbs, need I recount what
      labours

193

I went through? Lions, giants with three bodies, the four-
   hooved
Squadrons of Centaurs – all I fought and overcame.
The hydra too, swarming with heads that grew again,
I killed; finally, crowned a host of other toils
By invading the dark regions at Eurystheus' word
To capture the three-headed watchdog of the dead
And drag him up to earth. Now, for a last affliction,
I have topped our house of crime with murder of my sons.
No choice is left me. I am too much defiled to live
In my beloved Thebes. Even if I stayed, I could
Enter no temple, join no company of friends.
Cursed as I am, no one would dare to speak to me.
In Argos, then? It's Argos I am banished from.
Then must I try some other city? – and meet the glance
Of timid ill-will, a marked man, the prisoner
Of barbed allusions – 'Is not that the son of Zeus
Who killed his wife and children? He's not wanted here,
Plague take him!' To a man who has known happiness
Among his fellows, change is a most bitter thing.
A man settled in ill luck feels no pain; to him
Enduring it is second nature.

Oh, I see

What fate waits for me. Earth herself will speak, and cry,
'Don't touch me!' Sea will roar, 'Keep off!' and leaping
   streams.
I see myself – Ixion, driven round endlessly,
Chained to his wheel. Oh, better far that Hellas, where
I have been great and happy, should not see me thus.
Why should I live? What profit is there in a life
So beggared, so polluted? Now let Zeus's wife,
Glorious Hera, shake Olympus with her shoe,
Dancing for joy! She has achieved her heart's desire,
Toppling to earth, pedestal and all, the foremost man

Of Hellas. Who could pray to such a god? For spite
Towards Zeus, for jealousy of a woman's bed, she hurls
To ruin his country's saviour, innocent of wrong!

CHORUS: No other but the Queen of Heaven herself, as you
Have clearly seen, must be the cause of these events.

THESEUS: I understand all you have said; yet I cannot
Commend your wish to die, but rather counsel you
To live and suffer. No man lives unscathed by chance;
Nor, if we may believe the poets, does any god.
Have not gods joined in lawless love among themselves?
Dishonoured fatherhood with chains to gain a throne?
Yet they live in Olympus; and if they have sinned
They are not inconsolable. What's your defence
If you, a man, cry against Fate, while gods do not?

Well, then: obey the law, leave Thebes; and come with me
To Pallas' fortress, Athens. There I'll purify
Your hands from blood, provide you money and a house,
And give you those possessions which my citizens
Gave me when I had killed the Minotaur, and saved
Their fourteen children. Plots of land assigned to me
Throughout my country henceforth shall be yours, and
    while
You live shall bear your name. When you depart to death
The State of Athens shall revere your memory
With solemn sacrifice and monuments of stone.

Our citizens count it their pride to have a name
Among the Hellenes for help given to a brave man.
You saved my life. Now you need friends; then I will show
My gratitude. When the gods honour us, we have no need
Of friends. Divine help is enough – when it is given.

HERACLES: What you say of the gods is hardly relevant.
I don't believe gods tolerate unlawful love.
Those tales of chainings are unworthy; I never did

And never will accept them; nor that any god
Is tyrant of another. A god, if truly god,
Needs nothing. Those are poets' lamentable myths.

Yet even in this despair I have been pondering:
To kill myself would surely be a coward's act;
For one who cannot face the blows of Fate will quail
Before a spear held by a man. I will await
My death with patience; and I will come with you to Athens;
And for your generous gifts I thank you heartily.

Theseus, I know the taste of pain and weariness.
I've shirked nothing; never allowed my eyes a tear.
I little thought that I should come to tears at last.
We are slaves to Fortune; and we must accept our bonds.

Father, you see I am exiled from Thebes; you see
My hands are stained with my sons' blood. Then take their
    bodies,
Wrap them for burial; and place them in a grave,
And honour them with tears. The law forbids that I
Should do this for them. Lay them in their mother's arms,
Close to her breast, in that sad union I destroyed
Unknowing. When you have buried them, live on in Thebes,
And in your sadness make your heart find strength to bear
My sadness with me.

                    Children! I who gave you life
Have taken it from you. All my great and famous deeds,
The toil I spent to win for you an honoured life,
Your best inheritance – brought little good to you.
And you, my wife, so loyal to our love, which I
So cruelly have ended! All your faithful years
Of lonely waiting, thus repaid! What bitterness
For wife, for sons! To kiss – what sweetness, and what pain!

My bow! which I have loved, and lived with; and now
   loathe.
What shall I do – keep it, or let it go? This bow,
Hung at my side, will talk: 'With me you killed your wife
And children; keep me, and you keep their murderer!'
Shall I then keep and carry it? With what excuse?
And yet – disarmed of this, with which I did such deeds
As none in Hellas equalled, must I shamefully
Yield to my enemies and die? Never! This bow
Is anguish to me, yet I cannot part with it.

Theseus, I ask yet one more kindness: come with me
To Argos, and support my claim to my reward
For fetching Cerberus. I am afraid of loneliness
And grief together.

               Land of Cadmus, citizens
Of Thebes! Come all with shorn heads and in funeral dress;
Honour the burial of these children; with one voice
Mourn for the dead, and me; for we are all struck down,
Joined in one death by Fate and Hera's cruelty.
THESEUS: My suffering friend, stand up now: you have wept
   enough.
HERACLES: I cannot; I am rooted here.
THESEUS: Yes, even the strong
   Are crippled by misfortune.
HERACLES: Could I but stay here
   Changed to a rock that feels no sorrow!
THESEUS: Say no more.
   Give me your hand; I'll hold you.
HERACLES: No! Take care; my touch
   On your clothes means pollution.
THESEUS: Then wipe off on me
   All your uncleanness, all; I do not shrink from it.
HERACLES: I have no sons now; but I take you for my son.

THESEUS: Put your arm round my neck; lean on me as you go.

HERACLES: A yoke of friends – and one bowed in adversity.

– Father, here is the sort of friend a man should find!

AMPHITRYON: The land that bred him breeds a race of noble men.

HERACLES: Theseus, let me turn back; I want to see my sons.

THESEUS: Why? Can it still comfort your heart to look at them?

HERACLES: I want to see them; and to embrace my father too.

AMPHITRYON: My son, I am here; your wish is mine.

THESEUS: Come, Heracles, Have you forgotten all you once endured?

HERACLES: Nothing I ever faced before was like this agony.

THESEUS: Men will despise you if they see these woman's tears.

HERACLES: I live to hear you scorn me? Once, I think, you did not.

THESEUS: You invite scorn. Where is that Heracles of old?

HERACLES: When Hades held you prisoner, was *your* courage high?

THESEUS: No; all my spirit turned to utter weakness then.

HERACLES: And do you tell me I am crushed by suffering?

THESEUS: Lead on, then.

HERACLES: Farewell, father.

AMPHITRYON: Farewell, my dear son.

HERACLES: Bury my sons.

AMPHITRYON: I will. But who will bury me?

HERACLES: I will.

AMPHITRYON: You'll come back? When?

HERACLES: When you have buried them. I'll send to Thebes and fetch you back to Athens. Now, Take in their bodies, which the earth is loath to bear.

I, who have shamefully made destitute my house,
Will follow Theseus like a helpless wreck in tow.
If any man thinks wealth or power of greater worth
To him who has them, than a good friend – he is mad.

Exeunt.

CHORUS:

With mourning and with many tears we go;
For we today have lost our noblest friend.

NOTES

*

MEDEA

P. 17 *The Argo*. Jason was the son of Aeson, half-brother of Pelias king
of Iolcus in Thessaly. To get rid of Jason, who was a rival for his
throne, Pelias persuaded him to go to Colchis, at the Eastern
end of the Black Sea, and fetch the Golden Fleece. Jason sailed
to Colchis in the ship called Argo, and accomplished his task
with the help of Medea, daughter of the king of Colchis. Medea
drugged the dragon which guarded the treasure; and Jason
promised to marry her. They escaped, and Medea's brother
came with them. When the king pursued them, Medea killed
her brother, cut him in pieces, and threw him into the sea, so
that the king might be delayed by the necessity of recovering his
son's body. They eventually reached Iolcus. Here Medea con-
trived the murder of Pelias in the hope that Jason would succeed
him; but the people of Iolcus were indignant and expelled Jason
and Medea, who subsequently settled in Corinth.

P. 31 *The fire-breathing bulls*. The king of Colchis had required this
task of Jason, in return for his permission to seek the Golden
Fleece.

By his own daughters' hands. Medea persuaded the daughters of
Pelias that they could renew their father's youth by killing him
and boiling his flesh.

P. 41 *I'll anoint my gifts*. When does Medea do this? The action of the
play gives her no opportunity. The dress is brought in a casket,
and she sends it off without looking at it.

P. 56 *The blue Symplegades*. The 'Clashing Rocks' (already referred to
in line 2), near the mouth of the Bosporus, the gateway to the
Black Sea.

P. 58 *Battering at these doors*. The Greek apparently means 'battering
at these doors and unbarring them'. But the bars were certainly
on the inside, and Jason was calling for someone else to move
them. The word could also mean 'prizing them open with
levers'; but this involves further difficulties. So in the translation the second verb is omitted.

HECABE

P. 63 The more familiar form of the name, *Hecuba*, is a Latinism (perpetuated chiefly by the habit of quoting *Hamlet*) for which there seems to be no sufficient excuse.

P. 73 *No embarrassing appeal*. Literally, 'you have escaped my [appeal to] Zeus God of Suppliants'.

P. 76 The three Choral Odes in this play bear no relation to what happens to the main characters; they concern only the fate of the Chorus themselves, except for the last stanza of the second Ode, which reflects that suffering afflicts also the homes of the conquerors – a thought which occurs elsewhere in Euripides' Choruses, e.g., in *Helen* and *Andromache*.

P. 87 *Persuasion, queen of human arts*. A curious sentence. In Euripides' day many Athenians paid fees to sophists to teach them the art of persuasion. To make Hecabe look forward thus some seven centuries seems somewhat artificial to a modern reader. If Euripides' intention was to suggest the more primitive atmosphere of life in the Homeric age, why does he destroy this effect by the finished technique of Hecabe's speeches?

P. 88 *I still have one more argument*. Euripides probably does not intend by this passage to degrade the character of Hecabe. The revulsion which it would cost her to use such an argument is a measure of the intensity with which she desires her revenge.

P. 101 *The sea waits for you*. The extreme of suffering, especially with blindness added, was in the ancient world sometimes thought to confer the power of foreknowledge.

ELECTRA

P. 107 *The well is not so far away*. The Greek adds, 'from the halls'; and it is impossible to say whether the dignified epic word is used by the Peasant as a sarcastic reference to the meanness of his cottage, or whether such a use seemed to Euripides to be poetically suitable.

Do some harrowing. The Greek says, 'drive oxen to the field
P. 108 and sow my acres.' This sounds unconvincing. The word

'harrowing' has been substituted to make more sense for English readers.

P. 108 *And a shorn lock.* The customary offering made at a grave by the nearest of kin.

P. 110 *Bred on mountain milk.* i.e., he lives on a mountainside above the level at which vines will grow.

P. 111 *Look, friends!* Electra's first line is in fact, 'Alas, women! I break off my lamentations.' This is dramatically unspeakable in English; and is to be regarded (like many similar phrases in Greek drama) as performing the function of a stage-direction. Electra's silly terror at the sight of two men suggests a curious lack of dignity.

Crouching low. Here the Greek adds a word whose meaning is doubtful: either 'near the altar' or 'hostile to the house'. As the sense is complete without it, the word is omitted in the translation.

P. 117 *Men, bring all their . . .* Here the Peasant addresses two servants whom Orestes has brought with him. Later one of them re-appears as Messenger; see line 766.

P. 118 *By the way they act.* After this come five lines of doubtful genuineness, which are omitted in the translation: 'For such men govern their cities and homes well. But bodies of flesh without wit are mere statues in the market-place. Nor is the strong arm more steadfast in battle than the weak; this is a matter of inborn courage.'

P. 119 *To stuff their guts.* The phrase is deliberately rough; the word used for 'food' is one which regularly refers to the food of animals.

P. 121 *And some flowers.* This of course means garlands for guests to wear at the meal – still the regular practice in Euripides' time.

P. 122 *But there's one thing.* He means the neglect of Agamemnon's grave, where the usual tributes had been forbidden.

A lock of dark brown hair. It is not clear whether the Old Man has brought the hair with him. If he has, surely he has committed violation of the tomb? If on the other hand he is telling Electra to go to the grave, why has she not gone before, if such a thing is possible for her?

Softened with combing. The absurdity of this, after Electra has so emphasized the sorry state of her hair, supports the suggestion that here she is nervously rebutting what she both hopes and fears is the truth.

P. 123 *We can't be sure of it.* It seems probable that at this point a line or more has been lost. In the translation the words 'we can't . . . not wear' have been supplied to complete the sense.

Briskly. Another stage-direction which, in the original, is included in a speech – here in Electra's.

Belie it. The Greek says, 'are bad'. The Greek word for 'bad' can mean both 'of ignoble birth' and 'cowardly'. This double meaning can hardly be conveyed by one word in English.

P. 128 *Zeus! Conqueror . . .* These twelve lines are a formal invocation of divine powers. Orestes and Electra utter the prayers, the Old Man gives the responses. The first six lines are addressed to Powers above the earth; for the second six, addressed to Powers below the earth, the three probably kneel. It is a shortened form of the greatly extended invocation in Aeschylus' *Choephori.*

P. 133 *To run a mile.* Literally, 'to complete a double track in a horse-racing course'.

P. 135 *An honourable man.* Pylades was son of Strophius king of Phocis, in whose house Orestes had grown up.

P. 136 *He shows the head of Aegisthus.* It is not certain that the Greek implies that Orestes carries Aegisthus' head; but the last line of the Messenger's speech makes it probable. Otherwise, he simply points to the body.

P. 137 *Wealth makes unjust league . . .* The mixture of metaphors here is fairly closely translated.

P. 142 *I do not, in fact, exult . . .* After this sentence come two lines which, following some editors, I have transposed to come after line 1124: 'But why are you in this state . . .'

P. 143 *No expert in these matters.* The Greek word for 'expert' is probably a rather slang expression. If so, it would subtly indicate the attitude of the neurotic Electra to the whole subject of motherhood.

We are poor; we don't have friends. Another subtle sign of Electra's self-consciousness. Had she been a genuine poor woman she would have known what nonsense she was talking.

P. 145 *That beseeching cry.* i.e., Clytemnestra's last cry, which the Chorus heard.

P. 147 *The sword fell out of my hand.* It is a fine touch which reveals only now that Electra, who had claimed the killing of Clytemnestra as her privilege, at the critical moment failed and left the stroke to Orestes.

P. 149 *Loxias.* Another name for Phoebus, especially connected with his oracular function.

P. 152 *Now sailing to Sicily.* This seems to refer to the great Sicilian expedition which sailed from Athens in 415 B.C. The reference to 'blasphemers' may hint at Alcibiades.

HERACLES

P. 153 *Thebes.* Thebes is often referred to as 'the city of Cadmus', and the Thebans as 'Cadmeans'. In the translation 'Thebes' and 'Thebans' are generally used for the sake of clarity.

Whose bed welcomed Zeus. While Amphitryon was absent on a campaign against the Taphians, Zeus visited Alcmene in her husband's likeness, and thus begot Heracles.

The crop of Sown Men. Cadmus, founder of Thebes, sowed in the earth a dragon's teeth, from which sprang men fully armed. They fought each other till only a few remained; these became the first citizens of Thebes.

P. 154 *I killed Electryon.* Electryon was a king of Mycenae (or Argos) whom Amphitryon accidentally killed. Amphitryon, banished from Mycenae for this reason, was received in Thebes by Creon and there married Electryon's daughter Alcmene.

P. 155 *The Minyae.* A tribe in the neighbourhood of Thebes, which had formerly exacted tribute from the Thebans.

P. 159 *Pholoë.* A mountain in Arcadia.

P. 162 *If he's a rat.* The word here translated 'rat' means more literally 'awkward', 'one who does not know how to behave', 'no gentleman'. 'Boor', 'lout', or 'savage' might do, but all seem to lack the venom of contempt and hatred required here.

P. 164 *The huntress goddess.* Artemis.

P. 165 *He probed the inlets . . .* This refers to the story that Heracles cleared the sea of pirates. There is a good deal of variation in extant versions of the Twelve Labours. Why this one is referred to so obscurely, no word for 'pirate' being mentioned, is not clear.

P. 172 *Were you so near to death?* Literally, 'Did you stand so upon a razor's edge?'

P. 177 *Gold, with good fortune, yoked* . . . Euripides' contemporaries, familiar with the terms and experiences of chariot-racing, would easily follow the details of this compressed imagery. In a translation some expansion is necessary.

P. 178 *Me or Hera*. Throughout this short scene Iris is given the self-importance often derided by Euripides as typical of the servants of the great.

P. 182 *The knife and barley-meal*. Some of these details of sacrificial procedure appear also in the Messenger's speech in *Electra*. The knife, and the barley-meal with which the victim was to be sprinkled, were carried round the altar in a basket, while those present stood silent. A burning stick from the altar-fire was then dipped in water, and with this the people were sprinkled. These and other rites preceded the killing of the victim.

P. 195 *Yet they live in Olympus*. See the Introduction.

Their fourteen children. This refers to the seven youths and seven maidens who were sent from Athens to Crete each year as tribute, and offered to the Minotaur.

FOR THE BEST IN PAPERBACKS, LOOK FOR THE

In every corner of the world, on every subject under the sun, Penguins represent quality and variety – the very best in publishing today.

For complete information about books available from Penguin and how to order them, write to us at the appropriate address below. Please note that for copyright reasons the selection of books varies from country to country.

In the United Kingdom: For a complete list of books available from Penguin in the U.K., please write to *Dept EP, Penguin Books Ltd, Harmondsworth, Middlesex, UB7 0DA*

In the United States: For a complete list of books available from Penguin in the U.S., please write to *Dept BA, Viking Penguin, 299 Murray Hill Parkway, East Rutherford, New Jersey 07073*

In Canada: For a complete list of books available from Penguin in Canada, please write to *Penguin Books Canada Limited, 2801 John Street, Markham, Ontario L3R 1B4*

In Australia: For a complete list of books available from Penguin in Australia, please write to the *Marketing Department, Penguin Books Australia Ltd, P.O. Box 257, Ringwood, Victoria 3134*

In New Zealand: For a complete list of books available from Penguin in New Zealand, please write to the *Marketing Department, Penguin Books (N.Z.) Ltd, Private Bag, Takapuna, Auckland 9*

In India: For a complete list of books available from Penguin in India, please write to *Penguin Overseas Ltd, 706 Eros Apartments, 56 Nehru Place, New Delhi 110019*